John Sanders

John in his doctor's robe

John Sanders

Friend for Life

ALAN CHARTERS

First published in the United Kingdom in 2009 (hardback) by
The Choir Press

This paperback edition first published in 2011 by
The Choir Press

ISBN 978-0-9562190-3-9

Contents

Illustrations

*Unless otherwise stated, photographs are from John Sanders'
private collection.*

Foreword

by
Dr Roy Massey, MBE
Former Organist and Master of the Choristers,
Hereford Cathedral

I feel very honoured indeed to be asked to write a few words as a foreword to this biography of John Sanders. I fell under his spell while he was still assistant to Dr Herbert Sumsion at Gloucester in the 1950s and our friendship lasted until his untimely death in 2003 when I had the sad privilege of playing for his funeral. Our friendship deepened after I was appointed to Hereford Cathedral in 1974 and we became colleagues in the exciting world of the Three Choirs Festival during the last quarter of the twentieth century. He was enormously helpful to me when I was the new boy, and from his vantage point I really got to know the man and admire his consummate musicianship, his great gift for friendship and his wonderful ability to enthuse and instruct all sorts and conditions of men, women and children to make music to the highest possible standards. He was very much the right man in the right place at the right time and Sanders of Gloucester became a revered and much admired name in the hierarchy of cathedral musicians. We also gradually began to realise that here was a composer with an individual voice whose music was later to become part of the repertoire in many of the great choral foundations in this country and abroad.

The inhabitants of the organ lofts and choir stalls of Anglican cathedrals have for centuries been a significant influence on the cultural life of this country. Composers, organists and singers from time immemorial have served either cathedral or royal chapel, directing performances and enriching the repertoire of both sacred and secular music as they served their communities, developed their technique and instructed the next generation in the art and science of music. Consequently, the influence of church musicians on the musical life of Great Britain has for generations been of enormous consequence. In more recent times, radio, television, municipal orchestras, universities, conservatoires, colleges and schools have largely superseded the educational role of the Church as its impact on society has steadily declined so that in today's culture we could be forgiven for thinking that the cathedral organ loft has little more to say to the modern world. But nothing could be further from the truth. The cathedral organist is still a power in the land and a musical influence to be reckoned with.

In this age of specialisation the eclectic gifts of the chief musician of a diocese may, perhaps, be seen as an anachronism, but such versatility is a quality greatly to be desired. A cathedral organist must be choir trainer, choral society director, orchestral conductor, organist, accompanist, voice trainer, teacher, composer, administrator and, in the modern world, afraid of neither the mobile phone nor the computer nor a multitude of committee meetings. In his cathedral town and diocese he is inevitably the musical big fish in the little pond, and these demanding jobs have often been presided over by some of the outstanding musicians of their generation. The organists of the Three Choirs Festival cathedrals in particular have to demonstrate versatility in abundance together with huge expertise in coping annually

with challenging musical situations at the highest professional level of choral and orchestral conducting. John
Sanders was a genius in coping with the multitude of
demands made upon him as he presided so brilliantly over
the music-making at Gloucester for such a long period, and
this warm tribute by Alan Charters, for so many years a
colleague and friend, describes in affectionate detail the
career which was so outstandingly successful and enriched
the lives of so many.

I am so glad that this book has been written as not only a
picture of a remarkable man and a gifted musician, but also
a fascinating account of the musical aspects of life in a great
cathedral during a period of unprecedented development
and growth in the role of such places at the end of the twentieth century. It also adds some further insights into the
history of the Three Choirs Festival, that wonderful institution which dates back to 1715 and upon which John Sanders
had such a profound impact.

Acknowledgements

John Sanders would have been astonished to know that a vast crowd, many coming from considerable distances, attended his memorial service in Gloucester Cathedral. Perhaps he would be even more surprised to learn that every major daily newspaper, in addition to the musical press, carried an obituary of his life and work. Although he will be remembered through his music which is now being performed all over the English-speaking world, and a Sanders Society has been founded to promote all that John stood for, it seems necessary to preserve some account of his life and record of service to the Church and the music he made on its behalf. John would never have dreamed of writing his own biography. Behind the public performer was a quiet, modest and essentially humble man who gave himself unstintingly to producing the very best to the glory of God. This little book is offered as a tribute to a person who encouraged so many to give of their best and to enjoy doing so.

No biography can be written without a great deal of help from others. While researching this work I have been privileged to meet so many delightful people that it is impossible to name them all. Particularly memorable was a visit to

Chester where members of the choral society and the cathedral were so generous with their time and putting up with my insistent questions. In particular, Martin Cooke spared me valuable time with valuable information, remembered from forty years ago while he was in charge of the Chester Music Festival which was going on at the time. Janet Walker has been generous with photographs and memories along with Esther Noote, Ian Tirrett and others. The Chester Record Office was also most helpful in enabling me to track down relevant material. Philip Rushworth, the current organist at the cathedral, gave me access to records relating to John's time as well as showing me round the new song school.

For Three Choirs material I am most indebted to Dr Roy Massey for his entertaining and first-hand knowledge of the challenges and triumphs of the Three Choirs Festival and to Emrys Evans for his account of the earlier days when John was assistant organist in Gloucester.

For John's schooldays and university life, Mr Rod Hunter and Lieutenant General Sir Peter Beale have offered invaluable help, along with the archivist of Felsted School who dug out information which I would never have found.

I am also grateful to Miss Anna Turmeau for access to her dissertation on John Sanders' music and I hope this mention and the acknowledgement in the notes will compensate for not having been able to contact her personally. Readers will also recognise my debt to the book *Thee Choirs* by Anthony Boden, who generously allowed me to 'feel free' when quoting him. Also invaluable for the historical background to Gloucester's choir was Suzanne Eward's *No Fine but a Glass of Wine*. Another help in this respect was Dr Donald Hunt's *Samuel Sebastian Wesley*.

I would like to thank Bill Armiger for his help and encouragement as well as for casting a critical eye over the early stages of the book. But above all my thanks go to Janet Sanders who not only allowed me access to John's notes and correspondence but has given me unfailing encouragement with a great deal of patience for my efforts. It is to Janet and Jonathan and Anna that I respectfully dedicate this work.

Chapter One

The Early Years of Preparation

'I have to say this. He seemed such a decent chap I wanted to be his friend.'[1] Such was the first impression of a thirteen-year-old boy coming to Felsted School and meeting John Sanders for the first time in the summer term of 1947. And although they had different enthusiasms and interests, Rod Hunter and John remained close friends until John's untimely death. One is made to wonder how John Sanders developed such an eirenic and likeable nature, that through-out his life no one ever felt threatened by him and everyone found him such a totally trustworthy and sympathetic person.

His early upbringing was not without its uncertainties. John was born on 26th November 1933 in Wanstead, Essex to Mr and Mrs Mills. His father, who was a bank manager, died shortly after his birth and his mother later married Mr John Sanders, a structural engineer and widower with two children.[2] Soon after the marriage, John's surname was altered to Sanders so that he could feel a full member of his new family, which settled in Westcliff-on-Sea. Unlike many boys at the time he did not join a church choir as the family were Wesleyan Methodists and there was no place for children in the adult choir. However an early memory is that,

The young John

at the age of seven or eight, he would creep down to the church, unknown to anyone, and switch on the wind and play the organ.[3] It is a matter of conjecture how music and the organ came to fascinate him at an early age for there does not appear to have been any tradition of music-making or even appreciation in his family background. But in some ways these early years of the war were a golden age for many children who were not old enough to fully appreciate the seriousness of the situation. Parents were busy and were distracted by many forebodings and children enjoyed a freedom to roam and make new discoveries on their own or with friends so long as they were back home in time for meals. With John it was the excitement of discovering, on his own, the organ at the Methodist church. Many of us look back with a certain wonder at the freedom we enjoyed in spite of the warnings we were given by 'moaning Minnie', our name for the air-raid sirens which punctuated our daily lives.

But even in these days John's musical talent was spotted when his treble voice was discovered and he was invited to sing solos from time to time at the morning or evening services which he attended each week.

Shortly after the outbreak of war, John's stepfather arranged for him to go to Netherfield Preparatory School where the seeds of his future career may have been sown. The head teacher was Mrs Carrington, whose son and grandson were choral scholars at King's College, Cambridge.[4] The grandson eventually became a founding member of the King's Singers and a radio presenter on Radio Three. At this early age John was introduced to a lot of classical church music and it was Mrs Carrington who encouraged all her pupils to listen to the Carol Service from King's on Christmas Eve, directed by Harold Darke in the absence of Boris Ord, who was away on war service. At this time the radio was the main connection with the wider world and several million people listened to these programmes. In later years I was surprised to be told by two Germans who had been prisoners of war in the Canal Zone of Suez after the battle of El Alamain that they listened to a recorded broadcast of the King's service, along with their British guards, each year at Christmas time.

Schooldays at Felsted

In August 1943, Mr Sanders had decided that his stepson now required 'advanced tuition' and writing from County Hall, Essex in his role of Vice-Chairman of the County Council, asked the headmaster of Felsted if there was a possibility of John joining the school in the near future.

Felsted was founded in the village of that name during that great period of Tudor educational foundations in 1564, a few years after the accession of Queen Elizabeth I. In the twentieth century it had developed into a boarding school of some 400–500 pupils with a handful of day boys and a Junior School, founded in 1896 in the same grounds. Set in some seventy acres of beautiful countryside it had a well-established academic tradition and a great enthusiasm for hearty sports, which was common amongst the public schools and many grammar schools of the day.

But Mr Sanders had to face up to a difficulty in his desire to send his stepson to the same school as his son Frederick John, who had been at the school from 1925–29. The school had been evacuated to Herefordshire at the beginning of the war and the army had taken over the school grounds as a base from which to defend the country from the expected invasion. Mother, who is described as a 'down to earth cockney', was not anxious for John to leave home and was certainly not happy about his going to Herefordshire. She had good reason, quite apart from the maternal desire to keep her son under her wing. She knew well that she risked losing her son at this young age for the public and grammar schools of the time did not welcome interference from parents. The modern attitude of the right of parents to consult the school at all times and the right to attend parents' evenings to discuss the children's progress was a long way off. The school, and especially the housemaster, were very definitely *in loco parentis* and this right was often jealously guarded.

Mr Sanders wrote to the headmaster, 'Can you offer any suggestion to assist us to usefully bridge the period that may elapse pending the return of the school to its natural home?' The headmaster, who was fairly new, was not encouraging.

There was no immediate prospect of a return of the school to Essex. The army, now preparing for D-Day, was still solidly located in this convenient base and, in any case, German bombing raids on the east of England and the V1 rockets, the 'doodlebugs', were still making it unsafe for the boys to return to Essex. If he wanted John to go to Felsted School he must be prepared to send him down to Herefordshire.[5]

And so, in January 1944, John duly joined Form IIc of the Junior School at Canon Frome in Herefordshire, having convinced the headmaster that he was worthy of a place. During his interview with the headmaster following the entrance examination, John expressed his ambition to become a medical missionary. In Herefordshire the Junior School was separated by some twenty miles from the Senior School which was based at Goodrich Court near Ross-on-Wye.[6]

In Canon Frome John Sanders came under the influence of the Church of England for the first time and, although the preparatory school was in temporary accommodation with very limited resources, he was able to join the little choir which sang in the local parish church. John recalled with affection a Mrs Sprott who taught at the school in exile and returned to Felsted with the school at the end of the war. She taught music amongst other subjects and seems to have been the first to have recognised his keyboard ability. Although she herself played the organ 'with never a foot on the pedals' she was instrumental in encouraging John to play the organ in church and for school services. It is fairly certain that Mrs Sprott was the first person to give John an opportunity to learn the skill of accompaniment which is vital to the church organist and quite different from that of the solo player.

Felsted Senior School in 1945 continued the more or less

pre-war style of education although many of the masters brought with them more liberal attitudes as a result of their war service. Readers who attended public schools in these times will recognise the description of school life given by Rod Hunter:

> I thought it was great. Corporal punishment was still the order of the day, administered more by prefects than by schoolmasters. Indeed the only masters entitled to give a beating were the Headmaster and House Masters. School prefects needed permission from a boy's Housemaster before administering a beating and another prefect was required as a witness. A record had to be made in the School Prefects' Beating Book which included a column recording the offence. Two entries stick in my mind. Rationing still existed for a number of years after the war and this was perhaps the background to the record of a dozen or more boys being beaten on one occasion for which the entry read 'Illegal second and third helpings of cornflakes'. The other I recall left rather a lot to the imagination. It simply read 'Disgusting exhibition in dormitory'. I cannot recall John being beaten. I could be wrong but to the best of my recollection he was either a model pupil or knew how to keep out of trouble. I was beaten three times by David Waddell, my Head of House – who is still a frequent guest at my home and was also a fine musician – a horn player taught by Aubrey Brain.[7]

Many pupils of the public schools of this period react with wonderment at the charges of 'elitism' and 'privilege' brought against them by some commentators. They presented a far tougher regime to be coped with than the usual maintained day school and while a minority found it a harsh environment the vast majority, at least with hindsight, appreciated the 'tough but fair' regime. However an American, Howard Dean, who spent a year at Felsted in the 1960s and was an aspiring Democratic nominee for the United States presidential election, wrote an article in *The Times* in December 2003 in which he mentioned 'the rigorous regime of a cruel English public school'.

Above all, former pupils whom I have met agree that it was a place with something for everyone whatever their interests – the academic scholar, the sportsman and those seeking to develop their artistic gifts.

Many people who later developed significant talents can look back on a teacher who gave them their first encouragement towards their future career and in John's case, George Thorne exercised a real influence in several ways. George was nineteen when the First World War broke out and joined up in the Royal Army Medical Corps where he met and became a lifelong friend of Ralph Vaughan Williams. He spent some time in Greece on Mount Olympus but during a period of sick leave was posted back to Birmingham University, part of which was given over to the wounded. He remembered being invited to play the organ in the Great Hall there on the occasion of a visit from King George V and Queen Mary 'on condition that he knew how to play the National Anthem'! In order to enjoy a bit more excitement he joined the Royal Flying Corps and became a pilot, having trained in Oswestry, and later served in Ireland.

In 1919 George Thorne went up to Clare College, Cambridge as organ scholar to read French and music, and in 1922 went to Felsted as director of music. He married another keen musician, Elsie, in 1924 and the pair became noted for their generous hospitality to the boys and their enormous energy and vast enthusiasm in organising concerts and other activities in the school community.[8]

When John returned to Felsted in 1945, George Thorne was, in another musician's words, 'Kapelmeister', organist and choirmaster, conductor of the orchestra and the main keyboard teacher. He also had the benefit of returning to 'proper buildings, a chapel with an organ and all the facilities of a public school', although, according to one old boy, 'the army had left a few concrete shelters around the area'.

By this time John had been awarded a full music scholarship and had his first formal organ lessons with Miss Joan Wake Cleveland, who by happy coincidence had connections with Herbert Sumsion at Gloucester. In those days, and indeed until the 1990s, the King's School in Gloucester used to offer choristers free places for tuition, so a number of the cathedral choristers came from families with very modest incomes. Herbert Sumsion used to take the choristers for a camping holiday down to Somerset during the holidays and Miss Cleveland lived on the farm where the boys camped and she helped out with activities and arrangements. Years later Joan Cleveland used to come to the Three Choirs Festival, proud of the fact that she had taught John the first principles of keyboard playing. Thus it was that John Sanders got to know about Herbert Sumsion and Gloucester at the age of twelve or thirteen.

Another teacher for a while was Peter Godfrey, a former King's, Cambridge chorister and later choral scholar who was a distant relation of John's. He did not stay at Felsted and eventually emigrated to Australia and then New Zealand to become a major musical influence there as Professor of Music in Auckland University. I had the privilege of meeting him in the small town of Waikanae to the north of Wellington where he had trained the parish choir to sing Choral Evensong, using settings, canticles and anthems rarely heard outside cathedrals these days. Interestingly, he was invited to become organist and master of the choristers at Gloucester Cathedral after Sumsion but declined as he had already become established on the other side of the world. He did however bring his choir, the Dorian Singers, to perform at a Three Choirs Festival when John was director.

But the main influence was George Thorne who, according to one former pupil, David Waddell, 'discovered his strength as a first-class teacher of harmony and counterpoint with a scholarly interest in style, a knack for encouraging budding composers, and a pronounced aversion to jazz and swing'.

After the return to Felsted in 1945 George Thorne was able to perform works with which John was to become very familiar as a treble and then a bass in the school choir, like the *St John Passion* and Benjamin Britten's *Rejoice in the Lamb* with its complex rhythms. Thorne also founded a subscription Concert Club which attracted first-class performers to the school such as the Griller String Quartet, the Dennis Brain Wind Quintet and even the principal string and wind players of the Vienna Philharmonic Orchestra who, amongst other works, performed the Beethoven *Septet* and the Schubert *Octet*.

While at school John was already trying his hand at directing his own concerts as another contemporary, Peter (now Lieutenant General Sir Peter) Beale recalls. He remembers 'murdering Henry Purcell's counter-tenor duet *Sound the Trumpet*' in their arrangement for tenor and baritone voices, which 'was pleasing to very few of the musical cognoscenti let alone the philistines'. He also remembers John as 'appearing vastly senior to me', although they were the same age.[9]

And of course a musician like John could not avoid being made responsible for preparing his House for the annual music competition for which he was required to produce a programme consisting of a song sung by the whole House with two additional items 'of a vocal or instrumental nature' by an individual or small group. Again Rod Hunter remembers that when Gepps House performed their song the rest of the school were greatly entertained by the 'almost hilarious, athletic and energetic performance' which John gave when conducting. At the end he was 'covered in perspiration, with hair substantially dishevelled'.

Several fellow pupils recall that John developed physically quite early which gave him some advantages while in the Preparatory School and in the lower end of the Senior School. He was also a highly respected and popular boy in spite of the fact that no one can ever remember him being involved in field sports. During these years rugby football was the certain route to prestige and popularity, but John seems to have successfully avoided such encounters. However he did take part in some events and Rod Hunter recalls seeing a photograph of him winning the high jump at Prep School although 'he certainly did not pursue this in the Senior School'.

While it was difficult for a boy to avoid games completely, even in a fairly liberal boarding school there is evidence that, throughout his school career, John was 'persuaded' to take part in the House boxing competitions, as many of us were at the time. His close friend and contemporary Rod Hunter, who was himself a first-class boxer and was to gain a boxing Blue at Cambridge and then to become Universities Athletic Union featherweight champion, recalls that John once made a boy cry in the ring. And it is interesting to note that he was still boxing during his final year at school and on 14th November 1949, shortly before his sixteenth birthday, in the '9 stone 7lbs – 10 stone 6lbs' category, the school magazine records that 'J. D. Sanders beat Hadland in a hard but somewhat unskilful bout between two equally matched fighters who attacked each other throughout. Sanders won a points decision by a narrow margin.' He is recorded as having other bouts but the school records and magazines maintain a discreet silence about the outcome of the other contests. Although he denies any such activity I suspect that in addition to the 'encouragement' of his House Master, the school boxing captain Rod Hunter, may also have had an influence on his friend.

However as a music scholar, John was certainly excused the afternoon games which took place four or even five times a week. Rod Hunter has a fond memory of popping into the chapel with his games kit still on, to sit beside John at the organ while he continued his practice. 'When he felt like a break he would produce a packet of crisps (never rationed!) with the comment "This old organ has seen me eat a good many packets of crisps."'

Another compulsory activity in those days in which John was to play a full part was the Cadet Force, which had recently been converted from 'The Officers' Training Corps' to the 'Combined Cadet Force'. During these post-war years the school Cadet Force was a formidable institution, based almost entirely on military lines, and trained boys in military disciplines such as weapon training, fieldcraft, map reading and the ever-dreaded 'square bashing'. NCOs from the local military units would come each week to drill the boys and to teach them the use of the rifle and bren gun and many schools had their own twenty-five pounder field gun. The Cadet Force may have provided the first preparation for John's military service later on. He must have been a sufficiently adept and useful cadet, having passed his Certificate A, to have been made a Lance Corporal by the age of sixteen when most of the boys could not hope for such promotion until they were seventeen or eighteen.

John also took part in a number of school plays, including Agatha Christie's *Ten Little Nigger Boys* (the title of which has lately been changed to appease the consciences of a more tender age) and *The Amazing Dr Clitterhouse*, in which he played the part of Sergeant Bates, thus transferring his military endeavours to the gentler confines of the stage.[10] During these years there are few concert reviews in the school magazine which, like many other schools, concentrated on the exploits of the rugby and cricket teams in which John did not feature, although he is recorded as becoming Head Choir Prefect during his final year.

During school holidays and in later vacations, John kept up with his school friends and other boys often joined his family holidays with his mother and younger sister. However there was also the more serious business of earning a little extra money and during the summer holidays he worked as a deckchair attendant on the beaches of Westcliff and Southend. This would have been a more than usually demanding job as Southend was a popular seaside resort with numerous East Londoners who came by the coachload and trainload.

Another holiday activity which was much enjoyed by generations of young people in those days was sailing on the Norfolk Broads – before the waters became overcrowded and commercialised with motor boats. One incident is remembered when John, left in control of the boat, was approaching Wroxham bridge. Suddenly he shouted 'Stop the b----y boat', and abandoning wheel and sheets rushed to the stern and tried to release the dinghy they had been towing, before it was dismasted against the bridge. Alas he was too late and the crew suffered the indignity of a mastless sailing boat which was a not uncommon sight in those days.

That John was academically sound is witnessed by his results in the School Certificate examinations (precursor to GCE and GCSE) when he gained credits in English

Language, English Literature, French and Latin, and a distinction in Music. These were followed by the Higher Certificate at an early age in French and English – with another distinction in Music. This may appear to be a small number of subjects compared with later days but the practice then in many public and grammar schools was to enter only for subjects which were necessary. Many pupils going on to Higher Certificate would not bother to take the School Certificate and some who were bound for Oxford or Cambridge Scholarships would not bother with Highers. This principle was emphasised when O and A levels were introduced in the early 1950s and many talented pupils did not take O levels if they were going on to do the subject at A level, in order to prevent the examination system from becoming an obstacle to 'real' education. Alas the demand for bits of paper soon led to the abandonment of this excellent practical philosophy.

In any case John was awarded a scholarship to the Royal College of Music and being too young for military service, went there in 1950 at the age of sixteen.

Chapter Two

Professional Education

The Royal College of Music

On arrival at the Royal College John had the privilege of being taught by some of the most experienced music performers and teachers in the land. His organ teacher was the renowned John Dykes Bower.[1] Here was another connection with the city which John would come to regard as his home, for Dykes Bower was born in Gloucester, the son of a doctor Ernest Dykes Bower, who was ophthalmic surgeon to the General Infirmary and the school doctor of the King's School. Dykes Bower was one of four brothers who were all pupils of Sir Herbert Brewer, organist of Gloucester Cathedral, all of whom won organ scholarships to Oxford or Cambridge. John Dykes Bower himself gained a classical scholarship to Cheltenham College and eventually won an organ scholarship to Corpus Christi College, Cambridge, where he also held the John Stewart of Rannoch Scholarship in sacred music.

From Cambridge he went as organist to Truro Cathedral where, as recorded in *Grove's Dictionary of Music*, he 'enjoyed the exceptional privilege of working under a Bishop and Dean (W. H. Frere) who was a profound scholar of all that concerns the liturgical music of the church and particularly of plainsong'. Already Dykes Bower was marked out as a distinguished church musician and he held posts in succession at New College, Oxford – where he took an active part in university music and conducting the Oxford Harmonic Society – and then Durham Cathedral from 1933–36, where he played an important role in the newly formed School of English Church Music Society. After Durham he became organist of 'the parish church of the Empire', St Paul's Cathedral, and a professor at the Royal College of Music.

Dykes Bower was justly regarded as the most eminent organist of his day and one friend recalls being taught by him on the five manual organ of St Paul's and attending Choral Evensong in the organ loft afterwards. As the choir were processing out from the service, Dykes Bower asked Terry Gilmore-James to choose a piece of music from the great pile of music behind the organ seat as a voluntary to close the service. At random Terry chose a Rheinberger Sonata which Dykes Bower then placed on the music stand and proceeded to play faultlessly from start to finish, choosing exactly the right stops. It was an awesome experience for an organ pupil.

Another of John's teachers was William Lloyd Webber who taught harmony. He was also a church musician at All Saints, Margaret Street with a very fine choir and every opportunity of performing the greatest ecclesiastical music of Europe as it was a famous Tractarian church with a strong catholic tradition. In those days the main service of the day was High Mass, still rare in Anglican terminology. As elsewhere, worshippers who wished to receive Holy Communion were expected to attend the early Low Mass and only the infirm and elderly were permitted to receive Communion at the 11 a.m. service. It was thus an intensely devout, musical experience. It is not known how often John attended church there but he must have done so occasionally at least, and this would introduce him to a new and in many ways a more widely enriching experience from the worship of his school chapel and indeed his Methodist upbringing.

William Lloyd Webber was, of course, the father of two very eminent musicians, Julian the cellist and Andrew, composer of those world-famous musicals, *Cats*, *Phantom of the Opera* and others which have dominated the world's theatres for the past thirty or forty years.

John had a separate piano teacher, Edwin Benbow, who was strictly demanding and who also taught some composition. Years later he was to come across another Benbow who was a chorister at Gloucester Cathedral.

One of the advantages of the Royal College of Music was the opportunity of going to hear the finest orchestras and performers in the world. Students of the College were offered tickets at much reduced prices, or even free, to attend recitals and John would have extended his musical knowledge and awareness by attending concerts with fellow students and then discussing them afterwards, long into the evening.

While he was at the Royal College John found time, at the age of eighteen, to be director of the Southend Operatic Society which achieved very high standards in one of the favourite seaside resorts of the country. The production was Gilbert and Sullivan's *Yeomen of the Guard* and was well acclaimed in the local press. He also acted regularly as organist of St Saviour's Church, Westcliff, which was only a minute or two's walk from his home where he lived with his mother and two sisters, his stepfather having died some years before.

When the time came for him to leave the RCM, John was

still only eighteen, but now liable for National Service. But he decided that it would be better to go to university and on his own initiative, began to try for organ scholarships. The staff at the Royal College were not particularly encouraging. 'What do you want to go to Cambridge for?' asked the registrar. John replied that he wanted to gain a wider educational background. 'You can get that by sitting in the cafes in Paris,' was the reply.[2] Nevertheless John persisted. He was at first unsuccessful but showed a steady perseverance which overcame the temptation of becoming disheartened and finally, at his third attempt, gained the Organ Scholarship at Gonville and Caius College, Cambridge.

Cambridge Days

It was a happy success, for Caius College was one of the few colleges which awarded choral scholarships at that time and one of his former school friends had gained a choral scholarship and went up to Cambridge with John. Peter Beale had tried for and gained a choral scholarship at King's but when Boris Ord found that he intended to read medicine, he decided that medical studies and the demands of the King's choir were not compatible and recommended him to Caius instead.[3] One wonders at the justification of such a decision as I rowed for six afternoons a week as well as doing early morning training in a boat which contained three medical students, one of whom completed his medical tripos in two years and was able to study theology for a year before going on to his hospital training. Mike Hubbard went on to become a distinguished orthopaedic surgeon. Surely the life of a King's choral scholar need not preclude medical studies, demanding though it may be.

John came to Cambridge with a mature experience of his

subject, both academic and practical, which was not the case with many organ scholars who had come up straight from school. He also had a certain advantage over scholars who had come up to King's or St John's. They were under the guidance and jurisdiction of professional directors of music whose reputation largely depended on the quality of performance of their choirs and who would be less than willing to give their young scholars much responsibility.

At Caius, John had it both ways.[4] Although the college had its own director of music, Patrick Hadley, who was to become Professor of Music in the university, he did not interfere with the chapel music. Thus John was able to take a large part of the responsibility for running the music while having the extra joy of having genuine 'choral exhibitioners', several of whom were products of cathedral choirs and other excellent choral institutions. Other colleges were without music dons and depended for their music on a youthful organ scholar who had to muster what volunteer resources he could from within the college.

In those days the chapels were very well attended during the week when Evensong was sung before 'Hall', when all undergraduates sat down to dinner. On Sundays extra chairs had to be put out to seat the capacity congregations when chaplains tried to arrange well-known preachers from within and without the university and the choir was listened to with critical attention. John himself would have been one of the younger students as most undergraduates had completed their National Service, some for more than the obligatory two years, depending on the military circumstances of the day. However this never seemed to bother him as his contemporaries at school and university looked up to him and recognised his calm authority as well as his 'superb personality' at an early age.

The chapel choir, which consisted of altos, tenors and basses, as this was long before women were admitted to the men's colleges, rehearsed daily at 1.30 p.m. after lunch and sang choral services four times a week. This gave John an insight into the men's voice repertoire which would prove so useful later on when it was usual for men's voices to sing Evensong in the cathedrals once a week.

But of course this was not entirely to the liking of many men who at the age of twenty-two had spent all their lives in single-sex schools, followed by the female-starved armed forces and then in a university where there were twelve men for every woman. Caius with its high quality of music offered a glorious opportunity for women to sing in a choral society, performing the most popular music of the day, Gilbert and Sullivan.[5] Sopranos were recruited and auditioned by John for the 'Gonville and Caius G and S Society' from Girton and Newnham, as well as Homerton, which was the Teachers' Training College at the time. Peter Beale alleges that the ladies 'clamoured for front row places just in order to capture John's gaze or to be the butt of his kindly but some-times sarcastic humour'. Attendance was very strictly recorded and any who failed to turn up for rehearsals without good cause were summarily dismissed, shades of the rules later in the Gloucester Choral Society where the door was locked five minutes after the rehearsal was due to begin. Absence from twenty-five per cent of the rehearsals automatically debarred a singer from a concert. There are discs of recordings of excerpts of *Princess Ida*, the Overture to *Ruddigore* and *Trial by Jury* from this time, all of which bear listening to as well as a Musical Memoir of the Choral Exhibitioners of Gonville and Caius.

There was also a university Gilbert and Sullivan Orchestra which John conducted in which Roger Norrington played, 'athough he probably wouldn't like to be reminded of that these days'.

Several choral exhibitioners have told me that the women were most attentive in watching the beat and occasionally strong relationships were formed. In particular a girl called Pauline, also from Westcliffe-on-Sea, caught John's eye.[6] But these were days of necessarily innocent friendships before the age of maturity had been dropped from 21 to 18. In any case, all visitors had to be out of the college by ten o'clock each evening and the colleges were guarded by spikes on the walls and bars on the downstairs windows. 'Proctors and bulldogs', specified young dons and college porters, patrolled the streets of the city in their gowns and formal academic dress to apprehend misbehaving students and those outside after the ten o'clock curfew, although it has to be said that many ex-soldiers were adept at avoiding both the bulldogs and the spikes when they were scaling the college walls in the dead of the night.

John also conducted the Cambridge University Second Orchestra as well as madrigal groups and thus gained orchestral conducting experience which he would need later in his career. He once pointed out that there were also the King's and St John's choirs which sang daily services but he was so busy at Caius and with the university music that he rarely had time to go and hear them.

John stayed up at Cambridge for four years studying for his Bachelor of Music after the normal Bachelor of Arts under Patrick Hadley. Hadley had become a Cambridge legend in his own time, being a great character who had been wounded in the First World War and had a wooden leg. It was said that if he became exasperated when he was conducting the Cambridge Music Society, he would get out a knife and drive it into his leg – to the horror of the front-line sopranos. He was also alleged to be rather too fond of the bottle but was nevertheless a fine teacher of composition as well as being the composer of those lovely anthems, *My Beloved Spake* and the Christmas carol for treble voices *I Sing of a Maiden*. John was clearly helped by Hadley and some of his own work recalls memories of his lessons with the professor. Years later, during a meeting of the Campaign for the Traditional Choir, John told an affectionate story about his mentor, Paddy Hadley. He was asked why he had never written a setting of the *Magnificat*. Hadley's reply was that he found the text too difficult to stomach. 'Much too left wing,' he said. 'It's all right as far as "He hath filled the hungry with good things", but when we get to "The rich he hath sent empty away", I can't bear it any longer.'

Other contemporaries were men like Warlock and Moeran and John was also taught by Thurston Dart, the great authority on early music, and Hubert Middleton. John used to say that when he knew Middleton he was a bitter man for he thought he should have been elected Professor of Music instead of Hadley. While at Cambridge John continued to have lessons from Dykes Bower in London but he found that, by and large, he was his own mentor. 'We did an awful lot on our own,' he recalled, 'and it was what you did yourself that counted.' This belief that it was what you did yourself that counted was to become a firm principle of his life. It was in 1955 that he was awarded his Fellowship of the Royal College of Organists.

Some musicians have been inclined to complain that the university music courses are becoming too academic but this was not really so at Cambridge in the 1950s. Although music only became a formal Tripos B.A. Honours course in 1947, it was still an essentially practical course, training students to become church musicians. As Nicholas Marston, current Chairman of the Faculty Board of Music at Cambridge has said, 'One of the major shifts comparing then and now, or even thirty years ago, is from a course which – as its detractors might say – was intended above all to produce Kapellmeister, who were destined for cathedral organ lofts and able to write a good fugue or anthem, or a setting of the canticles, to something in which music scholarship – musicology – is much more central.'[7]

Thus by the time John left Cambridge, with second-class honours in both Part 1 and Part 2 of the tripos (at a time when first-class degrees were very rarely awarded) and the B. Mus, John had received a great deal of musical education from a variety of excellent and knowledgeable teachers and had been able to develop his skills as a director of chapel music and conductor of a choral society and orchestra as well as a keyboard player.

In the midst of all this activity in a crowded term, John volunteered to join the University Officers' Training Corps. Surprisingly this was a popular undergraduate activity, especially for those who had been commissioned during their National Service. They had to do three and a half years on the Army Reserve after their two years' service and for many this was a better option than being a 'Z' Emergency Reservist or joining a Territorial Army unit. The Korean War was over but there were still the final imperial adventures going on with Suez, a few weeks after John joined the army, Malaya, Cyprus, Aden and the Kenyan emergency. Joining the University OTC was a less risky business than taking your chance on the reserve.

John was naturally an 'other rank' during his OTC service which had professional army instructors, but it served him in good stead for his two years with the Colours. The Cambridge OTC was well staffed with professional soldiers such as Colonel Bentley, who was a graduate of St Catharine's College, the Adjutant Major Flanders and a Regimental Sergeant Major Snugh from the Brigade of Guards. Also remembered are Battery Sergeant Major Merriman who was 'a really lovely man' who instructed them in gunnery and Taffy the clerk who 'bore the burden of the worst stutter we had ever encountered'.[8]

Army Life

And so John was able to do his basic army training in two bouts of four weeks at 19 Training Regiment Royal Artillery at Oswestry during the long vacations, followed by two weeks on Salisbury Plain. Also, as potential officers, members of the OTC were able to take the War Office Selection Board (WOSB) tests at Barton Stacey in Hampshire while still at Cambridge. In many ways this training enabled John to miss a very worthwhile but sometimes uncomfortable experience, for National Servicemen who had joined up straight from public and grammar school then had to live in a barrack room with the majority who had left school at fourteen or fifteen and had a quite different life experience. Also those who did so and successfully attended WOSB during their basic training often had to endure sarcasm and occasional humiliation from corporals and sergeants while waiting to go on to Officer Cadet School.

The Selection Board procedures had been drawn up in about 1942 and were later copied by many companies and organisations seeking managerial candidates. On arrival candidates were seated in a hall and set an IQ test after which came a series of individual and team practical initiative tests such as getting forty-gallon oil drums over a seven-foot wall, an obstacle course and physical education tests.

Some time during the three days there was the requirement of giving a five-minute lecture on any subject of your choice. John's was on 'frying an egg' which must have gone down well.[9] At the end of it all the teams of eight had to sit around a barely decorated Nissen hut to await to selectors' decisions until one officer came in with eight envelopes. As they were passed round the heart was beating uncontrollably and one hardly dared look at one's neighbour, although strong friendships were made in those three days of working together. Those who passed travelled back to their units in a state of euphoria which was sometimes tempered by the attitude of some of the sergeants in the barracks when the news was announced. In my case a sergeant in the Suffolk Regiment where I did my training looked at me and said with resignation, 'Thank Gawd we got a Navy.'

But most people found National Service a worthwhile two-year interlude between studies or taking up a career.

John volunteered for the Royal Artillery, which seems scarcely the most appropriate regiment for a professional musician, having to put up with loud bangs and explosions as part of daily life and training. However it seems that many professional musicians found themselves in distinctly unmusical army units. I recall one particularly sensitive concert pianist of some note who spent two of the war years simulating tank noises and guns firing to scare off the Japanese troops in Burma, and two or three others who also spent their time in the Artillery.

After two weeks of National Service, John received the accolade of having the most brightly polished boots in the regiment. They were now due to move on to Mons, the Officer Cadet School at Aldershot, which trained officers for the Artillery, Signals and other technical units, as opposed to the infantry. However John, Rod Hunter (who had been with

John at Cambridge and in the army up to this point) and others were posted to a training regiment in Wales. John was furious and was not going to take this posting without protest. He telephoned Colonel Bentley at Cambridge telling him of the error. Within forty-eight hours the posting was changed and they were on their way to Mons. Four months later, John was commissioned as a second lieutenant.[10]

He then had a remarkably fortunate posting out to the British Army of the Rhine where he joined a Heavy Ack Ack Regiment in Delmenhorst, North Germany. By this time the peace treaty with West Germany had been signed, the army was no longer an army of occupation and things had become more relaxed.

Whether by accident or design John found himself in a regiment with a Commanding Officer, Colonel Warren, who was 'a music fanatic' and had organised a choral society. He immediately ordered John to become its conductor. John had no problems with attendance for, if anyone failed to turn up to rehearsals, be it the quartermaster or any senior rank, the colonel was on the phone the next morning asking 'Where were you?'[11]

Thus John was able to continue his conducting experience with a four-part choir, for the wives of the soldiers were happy to join such an activity which they might have found difficult in the local German community. There was also an attempt to start a garrison choir for the Sunday services but it fizzled out. This was a common problem. Earlier in another part of BAOR, the chaplain nearly despaired of maintaining a choir as he had to recruit two new singers every week to cover the men who were posted or demobbed.

The great thing about being in Germany, as John

explained, was that every town had its own opera house. He managed to get to the Bayreuth Festival, the Salzburg Festival and go to lots of other concerts as well. If he ever ventured into the Lutheran church for the Sunday services he would have found a great welcome and lots of Bach being sung. So his army experience proved to be a largely pleasant experience and even a valuable time for learning how to conduct and encourage an amateur choir with little musical knowledge.

As his National Service was drawing to a close, John applied for the post of assistant organist in Gloucester on the departure of Wally Ross to be organist of Derby Cathedral. He had already proved himself to be a first-class organist and choirmaster with a good deal of experience for such a young man, as well as being a meticulous and methodical organiser who left nothing to chance. He was successful, and such was his rare gift that the friends he had made at school, university and in the army were to become friends for life, even when he was totally occupied with the vocation he had prepared himself for, so thoroughly and resolutely.

Chapter Three

Apprenticeship

An army regiment is a closely-knit organisation in which there is a special quality of comradeship and mutual support, and on demobilisation many feel a certain sense of loss, however keen they are to get out to pursue their chosen career. On arrival in Gloucester however, John must have been conscious of joining a similarly tightly-knit community centred around the cathedral. In many ways the 1950s retained the last elements of a Victorian atmosphere and the cathedrals hung on to a significantly 'Trollopian' way of life. In fact John himself once said that in 1958 he found that the cathedral might be regarded as a private chapel for the benefit of the Close with occasional civic and diocesan services. For many years after the Second World War Gloucester had the reputation of being the least visited medieval cathedral in the country.

At this time too, the King's School was still small, with few boys in the Upper School and Sixth Form, although the dynamic and charismatic Tom Brown, headmaster from 1951, was busily reinvigorating the school after the difficult war years when the army had taken over Paddock House, then the main school building. Although originally from Hull, Tom Brown was educated at Westminster School,

another Benedictine cathedral school, and went on to Peter-
house, Cambridge, where he read Geography. After service
in the Royal Navy, mostly on Atlantic convoys during the war,
in which he attained the rank of Lieutenant Commander, he
spent six years at Clifton Preparatory school before coming
on to King's. He was a bachelor who attracted a young, able
and energetic staff of bachelors who lived in King's School
House in a 'rabbit warren of bedsits'. During these years a
great amount of building work was successfully carried out
and the school doubled its numbers to around 410 pupils.
The morale of the staff, all of whom came from Oxford and
Cambridge colleges, was high and at long last the school was
able to pay its teachers on the national Burnham scale.
Another former member of staff who joined the school
during these years and later became headmaster, Pat David,
wrote of Tom Brown, 'He had that presence about him
which is the hallmark of greatness; around him there was
always an atmosphere of excitement. Wherever Tom was,
things happened, sometimes amusing ones.'

Perhaps one may here be permitted an anecdote, not
quite relevant to our main subject but which illustrates the
flamboyant and optimistic nature of the school. In the mid-
Fifties the senior school debated the motion 'Smoking
should be allowed in school.' The headmaster himself
carried the day 'with an eloquent argument that smoking
might be made compulsory in order to swell the school tuck
shop profits'.[1] Autre temps, autre moeurs.

So John joined two rather distinct communities as Assistant Organist of the cathedral and Director of Music at the
school, both of which were governed by the Dean and
Chapter.[2] In the cathedral, the church services were
conducted strictly according to the Book of Common Prayer
of 1662 with Matins being the main Sunday morning service

with said Holy Communion at 8 a.m. and 12 noon except on the first Sunday of the month when there was a Sung Eucharist. Matins was no longer sung during the week but Evensong was sung daily, apart from Thursday, with men's voices on Monday and boys on Wednesday. On Friday the choir sang unaccompanied. The only sung weekday morning services were on saints' days when it was boys only. In some places, especially in choirs where the boys were educated in state-maintained schools, there was sometimes a difficulty raised by Her Majesty's Inspectors of Schools about removing children from classes in order to sing the Eucharist during school hours. Even in independent schools the inspectors were inclined to comment on their absence from class. But this was easily overcome by reference to the Schedule to the Act of Conformity relating to the Book of Common Prayer of 1662 which explicitly listed the many saints' days on which people were allowed leave of absence from their occupations in order to attend divine worship.

Unlike at most of the great cathedrals, the Gloucester choristers were always day boys and, in the Fifties and early Sixties usually came from within the confines of the city and were able to cycle to school quite easily. This had remained unchanged for many years after the Restoration and during the next two centuries, many of the choristers were the sons of lay clerks who had themselves been choristers and lived in the Close.

In the earlier days the lay clerks and their families had lived in 'Babylon' on the north-east side of the cathedral near Little Cloister. By all accounts it was an unhealthy, noisome environment which was adjacent to the stream which ran along the north side of the cathedral to Miller's Green to provide water for the millstream. It was also used as a sewer to get rid of effluent. A report of 1649 at the beginning of the Commonwealth describes the 'great old and ruinous building, the ground Chambers and lower part thereof commonly called the firmary and the Chambers over the same and upper part thereof commonly called Babylon wherein divers poor People that were heretofore and Singing Men belonging to the late Cathedral Church.' Later on these houses were described as 'slums' but the lay clerks were still required to live in them. Accounts reveal that they suffered much illness and disease. When a lay clerk could not find a home in the Close and was forced to live outside in the city, the Dean and Chapter gave him an allowance towards his rent.[3]

In such a closed and rather poorly paid community the lay clerks were notoriously badly behaved and the Dean and Chapter constantly had to attempt to discipline them. On one occasion it was necessary to decree that 'for avoydinge of night walking and scandal that may arise thereby Yt is ordered that noe member of the Quire whose habitation is within the precincts of this church shall be abrode in the citty or elsewhere after Tenne of the clock in the night'. Much of the discussion at Chapter meetings concerned the ill behaviour of the Singing Men who were fined one penny if they absented themselves from Holy Communion and threepence for missing sermons. Even when they did attend services their behaviour was not much better and two of the canons were forced to declare that, 'Whereas the service of God is much disturbed by such of the Quire that in time of devine prayers use to talke and iangle to their fellowes or others yt is therefore ordered that after warnings given by the Chaunter to such of the Quire as shall soe offend shall forfeit two pence which several offences shall be noted by the Chaunter.'[4]

For their part the lay clerks also had their grievances and

on one occasion in about 1696 they sent a 'humble petition' to the bishop in which they described themselves as 'having ever from their infancy beene bred up and served eyther as Choristers or Lay Clerks in the sayd Cathedral Church and by their constancy and diligence in the service of Almighty God therein they have bin diverted from and deprived of those advantages which their several professions or other opportunity of profit elsewhere might have afforded them'. They went on to plead that their salaries of £10 per year were 'very small and not sufficient for the maintenance of them' but they had 'nevertheless cheerfully applied themselves to the performance of their respective dutyes in hopes that upon the improvement of the Revenues of the sayd Church their sayd salaries would be augmented to such a competency as might render their lives comfortable unto them and keep them from the scorn and contempt which otherwise their poverty will of necessity bring upon themselves and their function'.

Organists too were often of an eccentric and idiosyncratic nature. One Stephen Jefferies was constantly being warned by the Dean and Chapter for his wayward conduct. On one occasion, when a lay clerk was attempting to sing a solo during the anthem at Matins, Jefferies shouted down from the organ loft in full hearing of the choir and congregation, 'He can't sing it.'[5] Another time he was accused of causing an 'unspeakeable scandal' after a Thanksgiving service for the safe arrival of William of Orange in 1688 when 'after Evening Prayer as soone as the last Amen was ended, in the presence and hearing of all the congregation (of some two thousand) ... on the organ plaid a common ballad, inasmuch that the young gentlewomen invited one another to dance'. However he was an able musician and composer and often received payments in addition to his £30 per annum salary for his trouble taken in copying anthems and services into music part-books. Several of his compositions have survived, including a Thanksgiving anthem written for 27th June 1706, a Coronation anthem and other anthems, *I Will Love Thee, O Lord*, *I Heard a Great Voice* and *Praise the Lord ye Servants*. Although these part-books are still in the possession of the Dean and Chapter the anthems are not sung today, but the cathedral chimes which still ring out from the tower three times every Friday were originally composed by Jefferies.

Life in the cathedral Close continued in much the same way during the eighteenth century with periodic attempts to instil more discipline and decorum into the choir. William Hine, who followed Jefferies as organist, is likely to have been the chorister of the same name at Magdalen College, Oxford and later a lay clerk until dismissed 'propter fornicationem, manifestam et scandalosam'.[6] He went on to study music under Jeremiah Clarke and came to Gloucester on the death of Jefferies in 1712. He married Alice, daughter of Abraham Rudhall who founded the great dynasty of Rudhalls the bell-founders whose work is still heard from many church towers over England and Wales today. The Rudhalls were all educated at the King's School, one or two of them having also been choristers.

Notwithstanding his early misdemeanours, William Hine was highly regarded in Gloucester for 'his skill in the heavenly art' and 'his gentlemanly qualities'. At one stage the Dean and Chapter increased his salary, a rare exercise of generosity, and it is certain that he was one of the leading instigators of the annual music meetings of the three cathedral choirs of Gloucester, Worcester and Hereford which became known as the Three Choirs Festival, the oldest choral music festival in the world. Although it is not known exactly when the meetings were inaugurated on a regular basis, it is certain that Hine and his counterpart at Hereford, Henry Hall, were close collaborators in arranging the meetings. Together they produced a joint Morning Service, the *Te Deum* by Hall and the *Jubilate* by Hine, later known as Hall & Hine in E flat.[7] It is also quite possible, as suggested by Anthony Boden in his excellent history of the Festival, that Hall and Hine discussed an annual meeting in 1709 when they met in Gloucester at what may have been the first meeting of the three Music Clubs. There had been a meeting of the three choirs in 1662, and it is recorded that there were meetings in Worcester in 1719, Hereford in 1720 and Gloucester in 1721, which suggests that the meetings were, by then, on a firm cyclical basis.

There is no record that the young choristers were as undisciplined as the lay clerks during these years although there is a record that the great headmaster, Maurice Wheeler, used to take his senior class down to the cathedral for their lessons when he could no longer put up with the noise of the junior boys coming from the other end of the schoolroom. But at least some of the choristers were high-minded young people for one chorister, George Whitefield (1714–1770) so disapproved of the Singing Canon who was a bit too fond of the bottle that, on going to Oxford, he found the company of John and Charles Wesley so much more congenial that he became one of the most notable Methodist preachers of his day.

Another notable organist in Gloucester during the next century who was to achieve world fame was Samuel Sebastian Wesley. On the death of John Arnott in 1865, the Dean and Chapter consulted Wesley about a successor and to their great delight, Wesley suggested himself. As one of the canons remarked, 'It was as if the Archbishop of Canterbury has applied for a Minor Canonry.'[8]

Wesley is certainly the best-known cathedral organist before the twentieth century, not least for his much-loved and much-sung anthem, *Blessed be the God and Father* which he composed during his three years at Hereford. Apparently he did not think much of the work at the time referring to it as 'a little thing to stop the gap and never meant for publication'. It is possible, as Donald Hunt suggests in his biography of Wesley, that his opinion may have been formed by the poor quality of its first performance on Easter Day 1834. At this time the men in the Hereford choir were in Holy Orders and lived in the buildings of the College of Vicars Choral. The collegiate regime had become very slack and they gradually took on the cure of souls in the city and local parishes and thus absented themselves on Easter Day, leaving the choristers and the Dean's butler to manage on their own.

Wesley's arrival in Gloucester was not auspicious. Donald Hunt relates a story of how Mrs Ellicot, the wife of the Bishop of Gloucester, invited him to meet and conduct a rehearsal of a Ladies' Society. Alas, after only a few moments of hearing them sing he banged down the lid of the piano and rushed out of the room shouting, 'Cats.'[9] He too had trouble with the cathedral organ which was in need of an overhaul and the quality of the choir was poor, having been allowed to deteriorate during the time of Dr Arnott, his predecessor who suffered poor health during his latter days.

John Sanders must have been aware that he was entering into an ancient and distinguished heritage which had enjoyed its colourful moments as well as the ups and downs in the routine of the daily services amongst moments of sublime excellence. He arrived at a time when the quality and discipline of the choir, as well as the canons, had been considerably improved and when two distinguished and influential organists, Sir Herbert Brewer and Dr Sumsion had been in charge for the previous half century.

There were however vestiges of the past. As in most ancient English cathedrals the lay clerks enjoyed a certain 'freehold' of appointment. They were provided with houses, had virtually no pension to look forward to on retirement and were reluctant to retire. As a result, as John Sanders remarked, 'There were some quite ancient lay clerks, and I don't think many demands were made on them as far as repertoire was concerned.'

However the repertoire was wider than John initially gave credit for, although a long way short of later days when he became fully in charge. Sixteenth-century music featured strongly in the daily offices and there was a fair amount of eighteenth-century music with a very large amount of late Victorian and Edwardian music. Modern music scarcely featured, apart from Dr Sumsion's own compositions like the well-known Evening Service in G major, the *Te Deum* in G and the B flat *Benedicite*. The Three Choirs Festival also had a profound influence on the repertoire, with David Will-cocks at Worcester and Meredith Davies at Hereford at the time, who both introduced a great deal of new music. Much that was learned for the festival was incorporated into the choral round.

The choristers too, were still recruited from a very limited area compared with most cathedrals whose boys were boarders. John recalled that the King's School did not attract the highest quality boys in those days as there were two excellent and long-established boys' grammar schools in the city. Although the choristers were given free education at the school, they 'were average town boys – some were academic, but generally they were slow learning'.

The five years spent in Gloucester helped John towards

the maturity he was to show during his appointment at Chester. However he was still an eligible young man. When he knocked on the door in Miller's Green to make himself known to the Sumsions, it was Alice, Herbert's American wife, who answered the door. 'My,' she said, 'you'll be in great demand for tennis parties!' On his arrival in Gloucester, Dr Sumsion, who had been organist for thirty years, gave John every opportunity to exercise his talents and encouraged him in his composing. In many ways Herbert, or as he preferred to be called John, Sumsion became his mentor and John greatly admired his musicianship, his calm manner and the excellence of his composing. He did once say that he wondered if Sumsion had ever intended to pursue a career as a cathedral musician as most of his early compositions were instrumental. Nevertheless his *Magnificat and Nunc Dimittis in G major* was a landmark which set the scene for much of the more modern church music at a time when it was a fairly circumscribed affair, dominated by eighteenth- and nineteenth-century composers, such as Boyce, Croft, Wesley and Stanford.

John was entrusted with the rehearsals and singing of the Friday and Saturday Evensongs and also conducted the St Cecilia Singers who rapidly gained a first-class reputation nationally as well as locally. They had been founded some years before by Donald Hunt, a Gloucester ex-chorister who became an assistant organist of the cathedral before going on to Leeds Parish Church and then Worcester Cathedral as organist. The Singers mostly sang unaccompanied but occasionally did concerts with orchestra and one of the highlights of Donald Hunt's time with them was the performance of Britten's newly composed *Missa Brevis*. Shortly after, they sang his *Flower Songs* which were broadcast on the BBC.

School music occupied much of John's time, for he taught a full timetable of music and trained the choir and orchestra. The advantage of a cathedral school is that there is a solid corps of trained voices with sight-reading expertise who can lead the lower parts while the current cathedral choristers take charge of the treble line. Other members of the choir can gain confidence from this body of choristers and ex-choristers and the result is often of an above average standard. School orchestras too benefited from the choristers' training.

In spite of a heavy workload lasting seven days a week during term time, John found time for composition and his *Festival Te Deum*, composed for the Cheltenham Bach Choir and published by Oxford University Press is still widely sung.

Some time before this he had written his anthem *My Beloved Spake* for the wedding of a college friend.

Looking back on his first years at Gloucester John was always grateful to Dr Sumsion for his wise training and encouragement. For his part, Dr Sumsion showed John his own compositions before performing them or having them published, inviting comments. Thus John heard Sumsion's *Evening Service in A* and a harvest anthem, *Fear Not, O Land* before anyone else. This was a great tribute from the older man as a sign of his respect and recognition of John's integrity.

Towards the end of his apprenticeship in Gloucester, John Sanders felt the need to grow a beard, perhaps to add gravitas to his appearance. On one visit to the Sumsions, Alice opened the door, looked in amazement and said, 'Gee, you've got a beard! Can I feel it? I've always wanted to feel a beard.'

But of course it was not all work at Gloucester. He was fortunate to live in the Close adjacent to his work and share much of these years with the young bachelor masters who had been appointed to the King's School by Tom Brown. One of them in particular became a good friend for the one year they shared together at the school. Emrys Evans was a graduate of Magdalen College, Oxford and knew the cathedral repertoire of those days very well, having attended Choral Evensong in the chapel on most evenings. As an amateur musician he used to play the harpsichord continuo in the school orchestra under John and the two shared a mutual interest.[10]

He remembers that John Sanders was immediately the most popular member of the Common Room as he had brought back from Germany a big black Opel car 'which looked a bit like the sort of thing Al Capone and his sidekicks terrorised Chicago with earlier in the century'. Apart from Tom Brown, John was the only member of the Common Room who owned a car. From time to time when they had a free afternoon, John and Emrys would go out into the Gloucestershire countryside together. In this way John became familiar with the surrounding landscape which he was to love so much in later years. A particular favourite haunt was the Forest of Dean where they used to leave the car at the Speech House Hotel in the middle of the forest, 'wilder and less well-presented for the tourist in those days' and go for a long walk among the trees, returning for afternoon tea. Other favourites centred on Tewkesbury and Deerhurst with its little Saxon church where they sang the Victorian tune to *Hark the Sound of Holy Voices* together on one quiet summer's afternoon. Peter Scott's newly established Wildfowl Trust at Slimbridge was also fairly regularly visited.

After five years in Gloucester, John felt it was time to take on more responsibility but in preparing for the future he had learned once again that lesson he had first learned at Cambridge: 'Whatever you have learned from others, it is what you do yourself that really counts.'

Chapter Four

Chester Interlude

Chester is one of the most beautiful cities in Britain. Although it has been rebuilt many times since the Roman occupation, when it was the headquarters of the 20th Valeria Victrix legion, architects and builders down the ages have always done their best to preserve its heritage. Thus the line of the Roman walls is still preserved and there is now a pleasant two-mile walk around the city some 39 feet above street level with outstanding views of the city and surrounding countryside. Within the city there is a whole series of black and white timbered houses, among them the 'Dutch Houses' dating from the seventeenth century and whole streets of nineteenth-century buildings, largely the work of two architects, John Douglas and T. M. Lockwood. Since the 1960s a large number of buildings dating from the thirteenth to the nineteenth centuries have been carefully restored, leaving the busy commercial centre with a strong sense of its past. When one thinks of the rape of other cities like Gloucester after the Second World War when so many historic buildings were torn down to make room for a ghastly shopping centre, one can only be grateful for the foresight of others.

Chester Cathedral

At the centre of this magnificent little city is the cathedral. On the site of an Anglo-Saxon church dedicated to St Werburgh, Hugh d'Avranches, the first Norman Earl of Chester decided to convert it into a Benedictine monastery and thus the abbey construction began. The abbey and monastic quarters, along with all the necessary trades buildings, were not long completed when Henry VIII dissolved the monastery. He found another use for it and like Gloucester, the abbey church became one of the 'New Foundation' cathedrals, in this case of the diocese of Chester. The king's statutes of the cathedral were similar to other foundations at the same time and provided for a Dean and Chapter and a school, led by a headmaster and usher, as well as provision for choristers. At first the choristers, who were members of the Foundation of the cathedral, were educated within the school but they had special privileges and obligations. All seven cathedral schools of former Benedictine Abbeys became known as the King's School. These seven King's Schools celebrated the four hundred and fiftieth anniversary of their foundation by Henry VIII at a great concert in the Royal Albert Hall in November 1991, meeting together for the first time in the presence of Her Majesty the Queen and the Duke of Edinburgh.

It was no wonder then that, at the retirement of Dr Middleton in 1963 from the organ of Chester Cathedral, there was a huge interest and response to the advertisement for a new Organist and Choirmaster. In fact, before the Dean and Chapter advertised, when it became known that the position was vacant, the Dean received several enquiries from several well-known and experienced organists. One of a selection of typical letters came from a justly famous former chorister and assistant organist of Chester, George Guest, Organist and Choirmaster at St John's College, Cambridge, on behalf of one of his students:

I am writing to you with a good deal of diffidence ... but I think I should always regret it if I kept silence.

[It is] common knowledge that Dr Middleton will resign as organist and ... if this news is true, I should like to place before you Mr Brian Runnett. I have known him for about eight years now, during the last three he has been my organ scholar here and I have worked with him daily. As an organist I should place him amongst the first half dozen in the country; as an accompanist, too, he is in the very front rank. But I think that it is in choir-training that he really excels. Maturity has brought a kindly but firm discipline, and it is this that has made him so conspicuously successful in this branch of the work. He is respected and admired by the whole choir and indeed by the College. In this field alone I am sure he would be the person to put the cathedral choir on its feet again.

As a person he is sensible and lacking in any tedious form

of temperament. He 'gets on' with everyone (even our present dean who, as you may know is not the easiest person with whom to work). He is a practising member of the Church of England and I believe his personal life is beyond reproach.[1]

This letter gives some indication of the competition which John was to face with his application. There were in fact some fifty firm applicants, most of whom had experience as assistant organists in cathedrals with their FRCO (Fellow of the Royal College of Organists) and many with experience as organ scholars at Oxford or Cambridge.

The Dean and Chapter laid down that no one over the age of forty-five should be appointed (in today's world such a requirement would be regarded as discriminatory), the implication being that they expected the successful applicant to stay for a long time as was the tradition in most cathedrals at this period.

Duties of the organist included playing for Matins, the Eucharist and Evensong on Sundays, Sung Matins on two mornings a week and Evensong on five evenings as well as taking full chorister practices each day and rehearsals for the lay clerks on Saturday mornings. The organist was also required to play at 'special' services such as those for the Mothers' Union, the Boy Scouts etc. and also for 'more important services' for which he would be paid an extra pound over the normal £4 4s 0d (£4.20) fee. He would also receive £1 10s 0d (£1.50) for taking the extra rehearsals. The going rate for weddings and funerals was £4 4s 0d, unless they were choral when there was an extra guinea paid. There is a note in the Dean and Chapter minutes that the salary of the organist would be £80 per annum with free house, rent and rates. Even for those times this seems very small and may be an error on the part of the chapter scribe. If that were truly the case the organist would need all the extra fees he could get, as well as the fees for 'private pupils for which there are excellent opportunities'. Boys at the Choir School, quite separate from the King's School at this time, would have to pay for their instrumental tuition and presumably the organist had a safe monopoly of keyboard teaching.[2]

The fact that John Sanders was appointed against such stiff competition is an early indicator of the impression he had already created as a first-class director of music in a cathedral setting. The sequel to George Guest's letter is rather tragic, for although Brian Runnett was not successful at Chester he was appointed at Norwich soon after. Tragically he was killed in a road accident a short time after his appointment.

After John was appointed, his tenure at Chester was by no means straightforward. The cathedral was broke, and one of the canonries had been suspended by the bishop in order to save money. The Choir School was by no means secure. Being quite separate from the King's School, it was forced to manage somehow on its own. Although it had eighty boys which is a reasonable number for a preparatory school, there were clearly difficulties in attracting staff. A new head-master soon found that the fee structure was unsustainable at £25 per term and this was soon doubled to £50. There seems to have been no reduction for choristers, although probationers were charged only £5 during their first term. Later the headmaster was in contact with the Dean and Chapter about the quality of the six full-time teaching staff: 'These men should have proper qualifications and experience, apart from the junior master whose main responsibilities are for physical education and games. The whole thing needs stiffening up by the recruitment of a keen and competent teacher who is interested in his work.' He went on to suggest that 'perhaps in future an assistant

Organist of Chester Cathedral

organist be appointed who might be capable and willing enough to undertake the teaching of academic subjects other than music'. And as George Guest hinted in his letter, the cathedral choir itself was performing somewhat below the standard expected of it. The 'bottom line' was that the financial situation was also desperate. Income in 1964 was £7858 0s 0d while expenditure was £8344 0s 6d.[3]

A solution to the Choir School problems and a help to the organisation and administration of the cathedral choir was found in the appointment of the Reverend J. Graham Canham, assistant chaplain of Ellesmere College, a Woodard School, as Chaplain Choral with some responsibility for the pastoral care of the choir as well as being chaplain and divinity master in the school. John would have to work closely with him during his time in Chester.

Another problem which John inherited, which must have been common amongst most cathedrals, was the now serious financial situation of the lay clerks. They approached the Dean asking for an increase in salary and also for a review of their commitments: 'It is becoming increasingly difficult to sing the morning services as it is necessary for us to find employment outside the cathedral.' Some of the lay clerks were past their best but 'it was very difficult to say to them, "I think it's time you retired," because you'd be throwing the chap out of his house too!'

Fairly soon after John's arrival, it was decided that the Eucharist and Matins on red-letter days should be sung by boys only. At the same time, possibly as a money-saving measure, it was decided that the choristers should discontinue the wearing of Eton suits and collars and that ruffs should be worn for services. As well as being an economy this may have been a modest acknowledgement of changing times and a move towards the relaxed atmosphere of the 'swinging Sixties'. How far John was involved in these changes is unclear for when he was back in Gloucester the choristers hung on to their Marlborough jackets until well into the Seventies. John's comment on the circumstances in Chester is characteristic: 'God didn't have as much money in Chester as he had in Gloucester.'

However the new organist did not appear to be in any way discouraged by the challenges he faced and one chorister's memory is of Monday morning practice always including new sight-reading exercises with new music. In this way the repertoire was steadily increased and improved. This was quite a change for previously the younger boys learned the music by ear from the older choristers and few of them could sight-read. They were not required to learn a musical instrument though several of them did so. Records of the music sung are missing although memories seem to suggest that Darke in F and Oldroyd in D was the staple diet of the Eucharist and there was a lot of Plainsong, while Evensong music was limited to five or six well-established settings. Also the choir had developed a tradition of singing everything very slowly. John was the first organist to conduct the choir for most services while the assistant played, partly in order to ensure that the music was kept up to speed. Previously, as in many choirs, the head and deputy choristers would conduct from either side of the choir.

Also of course there was not much incentive for a church musician to enliven the repertoire or compose new music at this time, for it was widely felt that the time had come for serious liturgical change to a Prayer Book which had remained more or less unaltered since 1662. In 1965 the Series 2, Holy Communion service was published and while it was widely but not universally welcomed, it remained a conservative, cautious revision offering little opportunity for major new works. Composers knew that change was in the air and were content to wait for the newer more radical revisions. This applied to the Roman Catholic Church as well, for the Second Vatican Council was taking place during these years. The prospect of the Mass becoming available in the vernacular after some 400 years of the Tridentine Rite caused many to wonder about the shape of things to come.

John felt rather frustrated with the cathedral music at Chester and that 'artistically the choir was in a bit of a strait-jacket'. It is probably true that all cathedral choirs had to undergo considerable change during the 1960s. However many have hung on to the well-loved 1662 Prayer Book services in the Anglican tradition and Chester Cathedral, along with Southwell, still sing choral Matins twice a month.

One area in which John thought he might make a difference to cathedral music was with the organ. This instrument had been built by the Whiteley Brothers of Chester in 1876 with a case designed by Sir Gilbert Scott. There was a major restoration in 1910 when William Hill and Son installed the electric action. Very full surveys of the organ were carried out by the firms of Walker and Son of Ruislip, Middlesex and by Rushworth and Dreaper of Liverpool, who had maintained it from time to time as necessary. Walkers suggested that the current organ was unsatisfactory in that the console was distant from the choir and went on to propose that the two main sections of the organ in the Transept and Chancel should be completely re-designed to provide two entirely separate instruments to be used quite independently of each other. The Transept organ should be a three manual organ – 'Great, Swell, Positive with 57 stops' and the Chancel or Choir organ should be two manual – Swell, Great with 12 stops. It is not known which specification John would have preferred as he had resigned before the project could get under way. It is possible that the Dean delayed the organ restoration until the cathedral bells had been restored and paid for. In any case the organ was restored when Roger Fisher became organist with the help of Sir John Dykes Bower in 1969/70, retaining the single console with its four manuals.[4]

The Chester Music Society

It is not unfair to say that John made his mark in Chester, not so much with the cathedral music but with the Music Society. At that time it met for rehearsals in the Assembly Rooms in the Town Hall, although sometimes use was made of the South Transept of the cathedral where the sound was better. However there was a quarter note delay between conductor's beat and organ which had to be overcome. Memorable to one member at least some forty years later was his first remark during the interval of the first rehearsal. 'I need a woman' – long pause while the chorus waited with a *frisson* of excitement – 'I am now living in the organist's house in Abbey Street and I would like someone to clean it.' Later his offhand remarks during rehearsals became legendary.[5]

Compared with most choral societies today, Chester enjoyed a strong body of young members, many of whom had just left school or, in some cases, were still in the Sixth Form. Esther Noot was slightly older when she joined the Society immediately after leaving college and was attracted to the pleasant but demanding atmosphere. Like many others she gained a love of the music and of singing in a disciplined society which has lasted a lifetime.

Another whose love of music and singing has lasted a life-time is Martin Cooke, current chairman of the Chester Summer Music Festival which John revived during his short stay. Martin had been a boarder at Haileybury and ISC, a school noted more for its rugby than its music but like most of the public schools of the day, it encouraged choral singing in chapel and for concerts. Martin had not been involved in Chester life during his school days, but as a young articled accountant went along to the Music Society to see what it would be like. 'John Sanders was the conductor. He was demanding and the rehearsals were quite intense. But he was a charismatic person who made us enjoy it and we wanted to be there on Thursday evening each week.'[6]

He had been going to rehearsals for some weeks when an older friend said, 'Come and have a drink with us afterwards.' When he arrived at The Ship and Turtle, there was John seated in the centre of the gathering. John invited him across and asked, 'Do you know everyone here?' and went on to introduce him and make him welcome. John not only loved a party – it was to become a feature of his later life in Gloucester – but he was also very alert and aware of the importance of making everyone feel at ease. 'He wanted us to enjoy the companionship as well as the singing.'

Such was John's popularity that the Music Society increased in number from about 50 to over 120 in his time and it is a tribute to his charisma and friendship that a Chester contingent attended the Three Choirs Festival from 1968 onwards and always enjoyed a party given by John and Janet during the week.

Martin Cooke related how he first really enjoyed his music and singing in the Chester Choir under John before he went off to London to pursue his career. There he was auditioned for the Bach Choir in which he sang for many years before returning to Chester.

There was of course another young member of the Music Society, the daughter of Len Dawson, its chairman. 'I noticed,' said John later, 'that there was a young soprano who was watching the beat perhaps more carefully than the others.' However it was not all straightforward, for in her teenage years, Janet had been captured by the sound of the Beatles, along with many other Sixties teenagers, and 'I was not too sure about that.' But it was not long before the engagement and wedding were announced and John and Janet married on 22nd July 1967, the beginning of what Roy Massey described as a 'marriage made in heaven'.

Although John was conductor only for a short time, the Society performed Bach's *St John Passion* and Mozart's *Requiem*, a new work for the choir. In April 1966 they were invited to take part in two programmes for ABC Television which included choruses from the *Messiah* and Haydn's *Creation*. Before that in March 1966 they performed

John and Janet's wedding

Mozart's *Mass in C* (*The Coronation Mass*) and Rossini's *Stabat Mater*. There is too, a memory of Bach's *Mass in B Minor* with John conducting. The organist had to transpose the whole Mass a semi-tone down as the Chester organ, which had not been attended to since 1925, was very sharp.[7]

John is remembered in Chester as a 'people person' who was more interested in conducting choirs and composing than in playing the organ and who always produced a pleasant and friendly atmosphere. This may have led him to revive the Chester Music Festival to run at the same time as the famous Chester Miracle Plays, dating from the Middle Ages.

The Chester Music Festival

The first Festival was on 23rd June 1772, when 'were performed in the Broad Aisle of the Cathedral, the cele-brated Oratorios of *Messiah*, *Samson* and *Judas Maccabaeus*, before a most polite and numerous audience. The several performers filled their respective departments with spirit and execution, and the amazing powers of the two Miss Linleys conspired to render the entertainment so great and excellent as can be expected, or ever was produced from the human voice.' On another evening a 'Concert of Select Musick' was presented in the Exchange Hall when Mr Linley junior played the violin.[8]

It was not until eleven years later, in 1783, that another Festival was attempted when works played in the cathedral were *Messiah*, *Jeptha* and *Judas Maccabaeus*. But this time it was more ambitious and the four days included other morning and evening concerts, a Fancy Dress Ball, an Assem-bly Ball and even a Public Breakfast. The orchestra was led by Thomas Cramer and the newspapers commented that 'so splendid an assemblage had not distinguished any similar meeting out of London'.

The Festival continued spasmodically during the next few decades with notable performances by Mrs Siddons at the Theatre Royal in 1788 and the visit of Thomas Greatorex, organist of Westminster Abbey, to conduct Haydn's *Creation* in 1806, 'a complete novelty'. By the early nineteenth century the Festival was attracting many celebrated musi-cians, including Robert Lindley, the cellist and the double bass player Domenico Dragonetti, whose dog Carlo always sat beside him on the stage. Its wide popularity is expressed in the receipts from concerts which amounted to over £3000 in 1806, rising to almost £5600 in 1821 when there were again performances of *The Creation, Judas Maccabaeus, Joshua* and Mozart's *Requiem*, as well as works by Pergolesi and Marcello. The *Chester Chronicle* at the time records that a certain Madame Camporese expressed her dissatisfaction with her treatment on this occasion 'after the very liberal treatment she experienced from the Committee, we believe she only gave five songs in the Church for which she had £150, enough in all common conscience one would have thought. The air of Italy, however, as connected with pecuniary matters, has unquestionably a bracing tendency.'

There was another very similar Festival in 1829 when Greatorex again came to conduct but then the bishop, with the Dean and Chapter, refused permission for the Cathedral to be used on account of the fact that secular concerts and a ball were held after the oratorio.

Famous names combined to revive the Festival in 1879 when the cathedral precentor, G. Hylton Stewart, and the organist, Dr Bridge, organised two Festival Services which included the lay clerks of Chester, York, Durham, Manchester, Worcester, Hereford and St Asaph with members of Westminster Abbey, St George's Chapel, Windsor and Leeds Parish Church also joining in. There were also two concerts in the town hall. At first there was considerable opposition from the ecclesiastical authorities but a campaign by a local newspaper, the *Chester Courant*, drew a lot of local support which eventually won the day.

As that occasion raised over £500 for the cathedral restoration, opposition was muted for the next few years and the Festival flourished under the patronage of the Queen and the Prince and Princess of Wales in 1885 when 'the City was brilliant with decorations, full of Americans and application for tickets came from places as far afield as Montreal and Gibraltar'. It had become, according to the *Chester*

Chronicle, 'a settled and perfected institution'.

With a new bishop who was an enthusiastic supporter, the Chester Triennial Festival seemed secure and indeed for the next few years it appeared to grow in stature. The Halle orchestra became involved and works by Dvorak (*Stabat Mater*), Handel (*Concertante in C*), Schubert's *Song of Miriam* and Gounod's *Messe Solonelle* were performed. The final concert of the series was in 1900 when Tchaikovsky's *Pathetique Symphony* and Berlioz's *Faust* began a most enterprising Festival, followed by the *Symphonie Funebre et Triomphale* by Berlioz, *The Deluge* by Saint-Saëns and other first performances by European composers.

Unhappily once again the church authorities were not happy with the music and the arrangements and were reluctant to allow use of the cathedral. As this had always been the centre of the Festival it was considered too difficult to carry on without the consent and support of the Church. Not for the first time had the church authorities succeeded in closing down a fine musical festival which attracted the enthusiasm and support of a large public and, sadly, it would not be the last.

It was a bold venture to attempt to revive a festival after so long a gap without an established committee. However, with the help of David Laing, manager of the London Mozart Players, who was appointed Festival Administrator, a programme of two weeks was arranged with the finest orchestras and world-famous soloists. Paul Tortelier appeared with the BBC Northern Symphony Orchestra under the baton of Constantin Silvestri, playing Strauss's *Don Quixote*, and later in a Family Concert with his wife Maud, another cellist, and their children Yan Pascal and Marie de la Pau who played the violin and piano. Tortelier also appeared with the Royal Philharmonic Orchestra playing Dvorak's *Cello Concerto* conducted by Silvestri and finally, conducted the London Mozart Players himself in what must have been an outstanding concert with his son Yan Pascal playing his father's *Violin Concerto* and Bach's *Brandenburg Concerto No. 4.* The concert was completed with Wagner's beautiful *Siegfried Idyll* and Mozart's *Symphony No 40 in G minor.*

Other music during the Festival included a concert by the London Bach Choir, in the wonderful Norman church of St John the Baptist, beside the Roman Amphitheatre, who performed Bach's *Singet dem Herrn* and his *Church Cantata No. 4* along with Schutz's *Magnificat* and Stravinsky's *Mass.* The Dowland Consort and the English Consort of Viola and the De Peyer Trio also gave concerts, the latter performing a work by Phyllis Tate which earned a comment in John Sanders' Festival notes, 'how unusual to have a feminine composer'. There was also an organ recital by the internationally known organist Jeanne Demessieux whose 'ability to tame the instrument; to liberate its various voices and make them utter not just sound, but sense' was praised by the *Chester Chronicle* reviewer. This concert proved to be a ground-breaking event in that the ban against clapping in the cathedral was lifted, or ignored, by the audience who showed their appreciation in a way that was unfamiliar in church up to this time.

The music festival was combined with the old established and famous Mystery Plays and it was also felt fitting that the cathedral should house the main large-scale orchestral concerts although the Town Hall was also used. Perhaps inspired by the Three Choirs Festival there was a concert by the three cathedral choirs of Chester, Manchester and Blackburn who sang music from the sixteenth to twentieth centuries comprising Purcell's *Funeral Music for Choir and*

Brass along with anthems by Byrd, Lassus, Weelkes, Wood, Harris and Stanford. The twentieth century was represented by Vaughan Williams' *O Lord Thou Hast Been our Refuge*, Randall Thompson's *Alleluia* and William Matthias' *O Sing Unto the Lord*.

Included in the Festival were a number of films shown in the Classic Cinema, craft displays and a Grand Festival Ball at which the Cheshire Regiment Dance band played and the final performance was the *Beating of Retreat* by the band of the Gloucestershire Regiment.

It was a formidable undertaking which was seen as a city event rather than a church undertaking but which must have given John important experience as a later director of the Three Choirs Festival. The cathedral choir took little part in the Festival apart from the opening service in the cathedral and the three choirs concert.

John is still remembered in Chester for his part in resur-recting the Chester Festival which is still going today, patronised by the city council, and the committee is now chaired by that member of the Choral Society who learned to love music under the direction of John Sanders.

The Festival was almost John's swansong for soon he was applying for the post vacated by Herbert Sumsion in Gloucester Cathedral. When he came to leave, Dean Addle-shaw was bitterly disappointed and was heard to grumble that 'Sanders only came up here to bide his time until Sumsion retired'. We know that is not the case for there was no guarantee that he would be selected and that, in fact, he was not the first choice. But John said that he 'was quite glad to be coming south again' for 'once you have had a taste of Gloucestershire you always look upon it as home'.

Chapter Five

Opus Dei

Dean Addleshaw of Chester was quite wrong when he thought that John had just taken the post at Chester as an intermediate step to returning to take charge in Gloucester. Nothing could be further from the truth. There was no certainty that he would be selected out of the numbers applying for the post and, in fact, one organist was approached and offered the job before any short-list was made. He was Peter Godfrey, chorister and lay clerk of King's College, Cambridge who had recently emigrated to New Zealand. The Dean of Gloucester, Seiriol Evans, who had himself been a choral scholar at King's, wanted a fellow King's man with the best of training for the post. Peter thought about it but decided that he had made his decision to go the Antipodes and was not persuaded to return. This was fortunate for the Charters family for in later years two of the grandchildren who had emigrated to New Zealand sang in the excellent village church choir under the retired Peter Godfrey and became used to the fun and excitement of taking part in a disciplined and demanding team of choristers who learned to sing sophisticated music, both liturgical and secular.

John had to go through the demanding mill of selection.

Later Dean Seiriol explained that part of his decision to appoint John was because of his genial personality and his ability to get on with everybody. This was vitally important in the rather claustrophobic atmosphere of the Cathedral Close. And so he took his place in a famous line of organists who also had the privilege and pressure of being Musical Director of the Three Choirs Festival every three years.

When John and his new wife arrived in Gloucester, he was returning to familiar territory and was used to the insular life of a cathedral close. Like any enclosed community it carries the danger of being a cohesive and exclusive society and there is a great temptation to become so involved with the daily routine and ordering of the place that the wider world is often forgotten or ignored. On taking charge John must have felt this, although he had the benefit of old friends from his earlier days as assistant organist and Director of Music at the King's School as well. He also accepted a quite different role as Director of Music at the Ladies' College in Cheltenham.

For Janet the prospect was even more demanding. Here was a new city and a totally new environment. While John was very quickly absorbed in the daily work of the cathedral, beginning at 8 a.m. and going on until 6.15 p.m. with at least two evening rehearsals a week with the Choral Society and the orchestral practice, Janet would have to make her own way and find her own position. For a wife, even a working wife, this is not the easiest of tasks as many a young wife knows. However she soon became an integral and essential part of the cathedral community in spite of very soon having the extra duty of bringing up their two young children, Jonathan and Anna, and pursuing her own career as a physiotherapist.

The first time many would meet Janet was at audition time

for choristers, members of the Choral Society and hopefuls for the Three Choirs Festival chorus. Auditions took place in the early years in the half-timbered house by what was known as the 'Tailor of Gloucester's Arch' and then in the organist's traditional house in Miller's Green, adjacent to the old Parliament building. On the house is a plaque recalling that it was once the dwelling of Samuel Sebastian Wesley, the greatest nineteenth-century organist. This would lead the aspirant to remember that it was also the home of the two organists who dominated the first seven decades of the twentieth century, Sir Herbert Brewer and Herbert Sumsion. So by the time the front door was reached, the heart was thumping, the throat suddenly went dry and there came a sensation that crossing the threshold of that illustrious building was an awesome experience in the full religious sense of the word. For most people the voice audition is the most terrifying experience they ever encounter.

But in answer to the hesitant ring on the bell there would be Janet, relaxed and smiling and ready to put you at ease. She was able to assess very quickly the individual needs, especially when auditions for the Choral Society and Three Choirs chorus were involved. Janet later admitted that when she went into John's study for auditions she felt every bit as nervous as the outside aspirants.

In the case of the choristers it was rather different. Many of the little boys of between seven and nine years old had never sung anything on their own before and were not sure what they were coming to. It was the parents who needed calming down with tender loving care and it was Janet who was there to give it.

Chorister trials took place on a Saturday morning when the Senior School had normal lessons but the Junior School was empty. It was a taxing day for young boys who had never had any tests before except within the familiar confines of their primary school. First the staff of the Junior School set them exercises in Mathematics and English to ensure that they would be able to cope with the demands of The King's School. They were then given free time to play and make friends with boys they had never met before and later to join their parents in the main school where they were given drinks and biscuits. Hopefully by this time they had been able to relax again and were then ready to go over to Miller's Green for the voice tests.

It was a fairly formidable experience, standing beside the grand piano with the cathedral organist, whom they had probably never met before, at the keyboard and three or four other men sitting around the room. Each applicant was asked to come prepared with a song or hymn to sing and this led to some very entertaining incidents arising from the choice. Then John would play a phrase on the piano and invite the singer to repeat it. He was always aware of the boy's nervousness and unfamiliarity with the experience and was especially patient with those who took a little time to grasp what was required. If the singing and the preliminary ear test were satisfactory he would then play a simple chord of thirds and fifths and invite the boy to pick out the middle note, or sometimes the lowest one. If a boy was confident he would increase the chord to five or even seven notes to see if he could pick out the middle note from those. As headmaster of the King's School, I was always present at these auditions, and I remember one small boy, whose father was a lay clerk, being tested with a chord of nine notes and asked to sing all nine in ascending order. He did it perfectly! In other words the able boy was tested as far as he could go so that some idea of his needs and ability could be assessed. That particular boy was to become an opera singer.

Finally, the applicant was asked to read a passage from the authorised version of the Bible, the purpose of which was to ascertain how well a future chorister would be able to read unfamiliar language while reading the notes of the music.

In a television programme about the choristers of the King's School John explained the purpose of the choral tests:

> First we are looking for a good academic standard, otherwise they would find it very difficult to cope with the work in the King's School while having the twenty hours' extra commitment each week as a chorister. Then it is important that they have a good musical ear to be able to pick up a wide selection of music quickly and accurately. They need to read well as they will often be confronted with the old English of the liturgical psalms as well as anthems in Latin or German.[1]

Chorister's audition. Seated left to right: Mark Lee, Canon Alan Dunstan and the Dean, Kenneth Jennings.

Until well into the 1990s only Gloucester and St Paul's, London of the fee-paying cathedral schools offered free places to choristers. And at Gloucester the ex-choristers remained in the Senior School on half fees, which was a considerable inducement. Unlike many cathedrals, even the sister Three Choirs Cathedrals of Hereford and Worcester until the last decade of the twentieth century, the Gloucester choristers were day boys, although soon after John's arrival they began to come from further afield. At first the choristers still lived within the city and would cycle or walk into school. As the school expanded and became more popular many choristers came from some distance which made extra demands on their parents who would have to fetch and carry them at times when they could not join a syndicate with parents of non-choristers as their hours were so different. One of the major factors in a boy being selected as a chorister was the willingness of the parent to commit themselves to driving to and from the cathedral seven days a week, including times during the school holidays when other boys were free. Services at Christmas, Holy Week and Easter and the Three Choirs Festival during August meant that holiday periods were strictly limited. The headmaster used to try and organise the school holidays as well as he could in favour of the choristers – this often meant extending the Christmas holiday well into January and as far as possible having the Spring holiday after Easter but other constraints made this difficult. The majority of parents in a school of well over six hundred pupils could and did object to the holidays being at different times from other children in their family for the benefit of the twenty-four choristers. Deciding on school term dates was one of the seldom noticed juggling acts to ensure that the choristers had at least some holiday.

Other factors too came into the selection of choristers. The attraction of free places in a fee-paying school led to larger than normal numbers of applicants. During the 1980s it was common to have twenty-four or twenty-five boys seeking three or four places. As a result some children had to be denied the opportunity of singing in a choir at a time when few parish churches were able to offer the experience. Sometimes this led to a boy being rejected in favour of another when he should not have been. On one particular occasion we heard a very pleasant and able boy sing quite well, although he appeared to have no real idea why he had come or what being a chorister involved. He was baptised and went to church regularly with his parents. We were puzzled by his ignorance until he was asked how many people attended the church he went to. 'I'm not quite sure,' he said, 'but when our family is away I think there is only the vicar and his wife.' The headmaster was delighted when, in spite of his missing a choristership, he came to the King's School where he became an excellent member of the choir and orchestra.

Another boy, whose parents were well-known professional musicians, appeared as an able, mature, confident and cheerful young man who was clearly a promising musician with a good singing voice. Having completed all the tests with flying colours he suddenly started telling us, with forthright honesty, all the reasons why he did not want to become a cathedral chorister. At the end John Sanders said, 'Well, I think I shall have to tell his mother and father that he shot himself in the foot very neatly.'

All the parents were told of the decisions as soon as possible after the trials and, in the case of those who were successful, there began a caring and concerned relationship with boys and parents thereafter. Each term after choristers joined the school John asked for their school reports so that he could measure their progress and see where he could encourage and sometimes protect them. He was amongst the best of 'housemasters' as well as being their choirmaster.

Once they became probationers, the boys were introduced to a quite new daily routine. Instead of the 9 a.m. start they would have to be in the cathedral song school at 8 a.m. for the first practice of the day. They would then attend lessons as normal, though missing the school's morning assembly in the cathedral. This was a fairly new routine for a few years before, the boys came to school at the normal time but missed the first lessons for their morning practice and sang Matins before coming into school lessons. The headmaster, Tom Brown, and the Dean had agreed that the choristers were missing too much school work and had instituted the new regime so that the boys could have a full day in school. For the first term or two, they would not attend the evening practices before Evensong until they had become fairly proficient and familiar with the order of service and the psalms as well as learning how to read the music of the anthems. John Sanders always said at the trials that he was not looking for trained voices as he preferred to train them himself. It was not until the early 1980s that probationers started to attend Evensong once a week in their scarlet cassocks after a new parent had suggested at a regular parents' meeting that the small boys did not understand what they were doing all this practice for and she thought it important that they should attend Evensong to become more involved and to discover what was required of them. Even then they sat separately from the main choir in a small stall under the Dean's eye. But this was in the halcyon days when there was no difficulty in recruiting choristers and when there was a full complement of sixteen choristers with six probationers in waiting. Today, although times have

changed, Gloucester Cathedral still has a full quota of choristers, although parents now pay half school fees. Some major
cathedrals are finding it more difficult to maintain numbers.

As probationers they soon realise that they have become
part of a well-developed hierarchy and they begin to have an
ambition to reach the next stage. After perhaps two terms
when they have become fairly proficient in knowing how to
sing the service and the psalms they are admitted as full
choristers in a little ceremony when the Dean or another
canon invests them with their surplice at Evensong. This is a
significant step not only for the choristers but also for their
parents who are now required to do more fetching and
carrying at often antisocial hours, especially on Saturdays
and Sundays. After another year or so they become
members of the Cathedral Foundation which consists of the
top eight boys. These are invested with medals which often
signify the origin of the donations to maintain the choristers.
Again this is a traditional ceremony with suitable words of
investment led by the Dean and Chapter, the senior
members of the Foundation. Finally, for the most able and
most senior, there is the responsibility of being Head Chorister. At the age of thirteen this is the equivalent of a
responsibility which other school pupils would not achieve
until they joined the Sixth Form and were appointed
prefects. There are also other duties which they take on as
they become more senior, one of the most important of
which is to lay out the music for the service in the stalls for
the men and boys before each service, finding the place in
Psalters and placing perhaps six different pieces of music in
their correct order. This is done under the watchful eyes of
congregation and visitors and so is a very public duty and
not normally a task which one would entrust to a twelve-
year-old without supervision.

Presented to the Queen in Miller's Green

One significant and interesting experience of a chorister reflects on John's strong sense of fairness and his avoidance of any hint of having favourites. At the beginning of the 1980s Jonathan Sanders was one of the most senior boys in the choir and everyone else considered him a natural Head Chorister. His father agonised over the appointment, fearful that it might bring a charge of favouritism for which Jonathan might suffer: 'My father did everything possible to prevent me becoming Head Chorister but in the end there was no one else.' In fact no one objected and Jonathan proved himself to be a natural, mature and loyal leader. At the end of his choristership he left the King's School to go on to Cheltenham College with a music scholarship and subsequently became a Choral Scholar at King's College, Cambridge. He remains a professional musician, teaching at the prestigious Hills Road Sixth Form College in Cambridge, with a large number of music students.

All this was the background to the daily routine of the *Opus Dei* which was so very close to John's heart. He was very keen to point out that the choir was continuing a routine and tradition which began with the medieval Benedictine monks who sang the daily offices themselves without any congregation, day in and day out. As he explained:

> It all began when this was a monastery and the monks sang their offices to the glory of God. We are continuing that tradition and it doesn't really matter whether there is anyone there or not. Of course on Sundays and at the major festivals the cathedral is crowded but very few people are there for the weekday services. But because we are singing good, beautiful and complicated music, it is important that we perform to a very high standard. I often think that, in addition to making an offering to the glory of God we are also offering a sacred concert from which everyone can get some inner enjoyment and benefit. The boys understand this and adopt a very professional air.

It is in the preparation, conduct and execution of these daily services that we catch a glimpse of John's own spirituality and faith. Like many educated Englishmen, personal expression of faith did not come easily to him and he was uneasy with overt displays of religious assurance and confidence from those of perhaps a more enthusiastically evangelical disposition. However there was always an air of quiet and peaceful devotion in his conduct of worship. He would have agreed with John Harrington Edwards in his book *God and Music* that 'music is a valid help toward meeting the imperative demand of human nature for absolute truth and imperishable love' and that 'along with many truthful witnesses to the verity of great belief the art of melodious and accordant sound bears strong confirmation of the

Christian Revelation'.² It is even possible that some 'who have no ear for Moses and the Prophets, nor for Christian apologists, may yet listen to the message of music, as it tells in clear and winning tones of the God of melody and harmony, who loves beauty and goodness with equal regard, and man most of all'.

John indeed had an ear for the words of the Bible and the liturgy which expressed the faith of the Church and was able to give them the fullest expression in the music. This was particularly apparent in the singing of the Psalms which in that beautifully numinous acoustic of Gloucester Cathedral with its special resonance, invariably led the casual worshipper into a realm far removed from the mundane stresses of normal daily life. Personally I found the 5.30 p.m. Evensong at the end of an often harassing and arduous day's work a releasing experience in which the cares and troubles of the day were taken care of in the reawakening of an aesthetic sense of a divine presence. One of the things I most appreciated about John's work was the way he used to bring out the meaning of the psalms and even give a godly sense to the most bloodcurdling passages, in particular his use of the pianissimo when reaching the climax of a passage which made you listen and meditate. He brought the psalms to new life each day.

He passed his own spirituality on to the boys as well as the congregation. One chorister, Andrew Wooldridge, a boy brought up in the Roman Catholic tradition, put it plainly when he said of John, 'He taught us that it would be silly to sing such things about God and Jesus Christ if we did not believe in them.' And echoing other choristers, he added, 'But I think as well as singing for the glory of God we also sing for John Sanders.'³

In his earlier days, John would become irritated and angry

with a chorister whom he felt was not pulling his weight or attending. There was one memorable occasion in the middle of a service when he marched over to a boy and almost lifted him out of the choir stalls with frustration. However he soon became known as a gentle and eirenic teacher who was more than patient. He would not put up with slovenly artic-ulation or any sloppiness. Frequently he would upbraid the boys in practice for 'nasty vowels' and one, Andrew Gardner, recalls that to make a mistake when singing a passage which had been well rehearsed 'was a punishable offence'. In his later years at least, the worst punishment a chorister would experience was the feeling of having let the side down. As Mark Blatchly wrote, 'About once a term John would be distracted by an inattentive chorister and break his genial discourse in mid-sentence and shout at the offender: "You're the sort who's going to muck it all up." The whole choir would jump and corporately resolve to double its efforts. John, oblivious to the stir he had created, would resume as if nothing had happened.' This was a characteris-tic which followed him throughout his life. He was constantly making remarks which convulsed his audience, to which he would respond by saying, 'Have I said something?' I experienced one small surprise when, in the early 1980s, corporal punishment was abolished in the King's School, before when it had been in fairly frequent use. John came and said to the headmaster, 'I suppose I will have to get rid of my cane now.' I was not sure if he was joking but the choristers assured me that there was one lying in a corner of the song school.

The Master of the Choristers also had disagreeable moments. Cathedral choristers have always been an attrac-tion for the less desirable members of society and the Gloucester boys were no exception. In the space of two years three incidents come to mind illustrating the diligence which needed to be maintained. On one occasion when leaving the school where they did their homework before evening choir practice at 5 p.m., two boys who were a little behind the others were molested by a man lurking in the cloisters. Fortunately John had come to look for them to hurry them up and saved a very unpleasant situation.

Another was more sinister and was a salutary reminder of the need for vigilance against predators seeking out victims amongst young choristers. After school, the choristers were given tea and cakes in the dining hall and then supervised for some homework before choir practice. Inevitably there was a gap when they collected their books and bags and made their way to the cathedral. One afternoon a young chorister was walking along the street towards the cathedral when a car drew up and two men leapt out brandishing cards, saying they were taking him to the police station for questioning. With real presence of mind, Robin took to his heels and ran to the Senior School and reported it to the headmaster who rang the police. As always when young children were involved the police appeared within minutes. Robin was able to tell them what sort of car it was and gave them some description of the men (it was perhaps a happy accident that the men had chosen a victim whose father was a police inspector and his mother a police sergeant). Later the police were able to report that the men in question had been arrested in Kidderminster, some forty miles from Gloucester, and that they were already wanted for questioning about an incident in Exeter Cathedral.

A third incident nearly caught everyone off-guard. On Saturday afternoons Evensong is at 4 p.m. which means that the choristers were unable to take part in school matches. It was arranged that they should enjoy a 'choristers' recreation' in King's School House supervised by my wife Frances and just before they left for the practice would have drinks and cake and biscuits. At times it may have added to Frances' grey hairs but on the whole it was a time of relaxation enjoyed by all. A man who may not have known about the choristers' supervision between morning school and Evensong, started coming to the Saturday service wearing a Master of Arts gown. He seemed a knowledgeable and pleasant person who told us how he loved Choral Evensong and made a point of coming to Gloucester on Saturdays to hear it. He explained that he was headmaster of a well-known Preparatory School in the Midlands. After some weeks he brought packets of sweets, pens and pencils with him which, with permission, he gave to the choristers after the service. A few weeks later he asked the organist if he could invite two or three of the boys out to tea. John said that they already had tea and that such an invitation would be inappropriate. He asked the headmaster to telephone the man at his school, which he did the following Monday. The headmaster of the Preparatory School was astonished and said he had never been to Gloucester in his life and had certainly never attended Evensong! He asked us to apprehend the impersonator. The mysterious thing was that the man never appeared again. How did he know that he had been rumbled?

Such events are a reminder that anyone responsible for children *in loco parentis* and especially a choirmaster who inevitably has a special responsibility, has to be alert for a wide range of eventualities. These situations arose shortly before the passing of The Children Act and were a warning that no act of parliament can safeguard young people without the utmost diligence of those concerned in their welfare.

Another important aspect of the choristers' life in which the Master of the Choristers had a vital role was that of

chorister recreation and entertainment. As a reward for
efforts over Christmas there was always an annual outing to
the pantomime accompanied by Janet and their children. As
Jonathan and Anna grew older and no longer wanted to join
the younger choristers at the pantomime it was left to others
to supervise the arrangement with John. On one occasion
when the choristers themselves had chosen the venue,
largely because some of their favourite television artists
were playing leading parts, I recall that John became so
bored with the production that he pulled out a book and
was reading it with the aid of a tiny torch, quite oblivious to
the audience participation around him.

But the highlight of the year was the choristers' seven-a-
side rugby competition where the Western Division schools
met for a knock-out tournament. It continued for a few years
competitively but amiably until some alarm was raised about
the unequal terms under which some of the teams were
expected to play. If there was a young choir, the boys might
be aged ten or eleven while a choir with mature trebles
might have thirteen- and fourteen-year-olds playing for
them. On one occasion Douglas and Alexander Mason, then
aged about twelve and ten, complained that 'some of the
boys in the Worcester team are speaking with bass voices'.
The days of the rugby matches came to an end in the 1980s
when it was realised that the age difference was potentially
dangerous and the event became a five-a-side soccer competition. It was just as well, for on the final rugby occasion
when the hosts were Hereford, two of the Gloucester team
ended up in the County Hospital with broken limbs. Fortunately on that occasion there was not only John Sanders but
also Geoffrey Johnston, a King's schoolmaster, and the headmaster present to be with the boys in hospital and to drive
the minibus home.

In the 1980s, as mentioned, my wife Frances was the volunteer who supervised Saturday 'choristers' recreation' in King's School House. It became an occasion when the boys, recovering from a strictly disciplined regime during the rest of the week, could let their hair down. All sorts of noisy activities were invented, including one occasion when a scheme to electrify an old harmonium by adapting a vacuum cleaner motor to the bellows was tried. All went well until the motor was switched on and it was found that it made a deafeningly shrill sound which drowned any notes played on the keyboard. The real fear of the day was that the boys would make so much noise that they would lose their voices before the rehearsal for the service. As a result of Frances' experience of being left in charge of the choristers it was once decided that, in the absence of the Master of the Choristers and the headmaster, she would be responsible for taking the boys to one of the Western Division chorister football competitions in Bristol with one or two mothers. After their return one mother was heard to say, 'Never again will I allow Frances to be put under that duress!' She did become very attached to those choristers and has since followed their careers with great interest.

The 1980s probably revealed most graphically John's skill and encouragement as a teacher. During those years a good many choristers found their life's vocation in music. Two decades later it was found that sixty per cent of the boys had taken up music as their profession. Among them were Nicholas O'Neill who had gained his FRCO while still at school and Alexander Mason who achieved his ARCO (Associate of the Royal College of Organists) at the same time. Alexander, during his time as a chorister, was winner of the annual Choristers' Composition Competition judged by Professor Kenneth Leighton. Both are now established cathedral organists – having been organ scholars at Magdalen College, Oxford and Worcester College, Oxford respectively – Nicholas at St George's Roman Catholic Cathedral, Southwark and Alexander at St David's. Several others, among them Andrew Stratford (Stratty to his fellows), are now directors of music in various schools while another has become an internationally renowned percussionist who travels the world playing for the musical *Les Miserables*. John would have been extremely proud to know that another of those choristers has achieved the highest distinction by becoming Director of the English National Opera in Covent Garden at the age of thirty-two. Edward Gardner (Eddy to his friends) went on to Eton College as a scholar after leaving the choir at a time when an outstanding music tradition had been developed there. Like Jonathan Sanders he became a Choral Scholar at King's, Cambridge and his career developed into opera from there.

Along with John's leadership of the cathedral choir and his individual teaching, the King's School was fortunate to have Ian Fox, formerly assistant organist in Chichester Cathedral, as Director of Music. As well as teaching the choristers music theory one period each week he also played an important part in encouraging their instrumental playing and directing the school choir in which ex-choristers took a prominent role in leading the lower parts. We were all a bit fearful of Ian's occasional explosions when he felt things were not going right. One unforgettable moment came when I was attempting to play the trombone in the orchestra, when Ian suddenly stopped conducting and marched over to the clarinet section where Eddy Gardner was at the desk. He obviously felt that Eddy had been less than attentive and leaned over him, glowering angrily while Eddy's clarinet was frozen to his lips.

But enough of the choristers, for whom there was an established precedent dating back some four hundred years as part of the Foundation. The lay clerks were also a vital part of the choir who were in effect paid employees. As we have seen they were often ageing men who had seen better days but because of their status and freehold in the Close, could not easily be retired. Fortunately for John the dynamic Dean, Seiriol Evans, himself a keen musician and ex-choral scholar of King's College, Cambridge, realised that something had to be done. He had started to replace the men in the early Sixties and John found the standards very much better than when he was assistant. The first incomer with a choral-scholar type employment was Barrie Thompson, direct from a choral scholarship at Selwyn College, Cambridge, who was to be a stalwart in the bass section until the 1990s, as well as a master at the King's School, completing his time there as head of the Middle School department. Another appointment was Michael Gillions, an erstwhile Choral Scholar at Christ Church, Oxford, who strengthened the tenor section. Shortly after John's arrival a replacement alto was found and then Bill Armiger came in as another bass with a strong musical background and training. Bill recalled his audition with John some forty years later when, after singing *Locus este* and a Finzi song, John said 'Very nice but have you got something quiet?' He is still very much in demand as a soloist and has rejoined the cathedral choir after retiring in 2005. It was not long until the main choir had a team of highly trained musicians with very good voices in the lower parts. Alongside the men came a definite improvement in the boys who, as the status of the school improved, tended to be brighter on entry.

There is no doubt that John commanded respect and admiration from the whole choir as well as a deep personal friendship although, as Bill Armiger says, 'they always knew who was boss'. It is not always appreciated that lay clerks need to be handled very carefully at times. Unlike former days their salaries were nowhere near sufficient to support them and all had other, often demanding jobs which made great demands. Yet at 5 p.m. during their brief rehearsal for Evensong they had to become professional singers to produce perfectly satisfying music for the glory of God. During John's time the lay clerks came from a variety of occupations, amongst them schoolmasters, insurance assessors, professional music teachers, a member of GCHQ, the government intelligence gathering agency, and local government officers. Weekends had little meaning for them as they were required to attend a Saturday morning practice as well as 4 p.m. Evensong and then two major services on the Sunday. In addition much of their summer was taken up with Three Choirs rehearsals which demanded an even higher standard of performance. It was no easy task for the choirmaster to maintain a rigorous quality while understanding the enormous pressures which all lay clerks would experience at some time or other. Perhaps John's main gift to the choir was that he gave the whole choir a pride in their work and a sense of joy in their achievement of excellence. His passion for accuracy of rhythm, diction, pitch and expression became legendary and while he sometimes might display a frustration with 'nasty' or 'sour' words, he would never humiliate. He was a natural and brilliant teacher.

His whole approach was summed up in a brief comment over the telephone by a lay clerk who spent a year in the choir during John's last year. John Brooks, a professional musician, organist and choir director in the United States, spoke of the 'thrilling and marvellous experience to be at the receiving end of his expertise. Every rehearsal was a master-class carried out with a fabulous sense of dry and witty humour. Yet he was also very self-effacing. With his soft-spoken approach, his enthusiasm for his work spilled over into the kids who thoroughly enjoyed being there with him. He had a modest and sterling quality about him.'[4] Roy Massey added to this assessment: 'John transformed the musical standards and repertoire of the cathedral choir who loved his genial but demanding rehearsal technique and the visiting orchestras respected his musicianship and clarity of direction. His relaxed manner hid a quiet determination to have things exactly right. It was all done with a lightness of touch and a warm humanity and humility which endeared him to everyone.'

The improved quality of the choristers and the lay clerks obviously made a significant difference to the music of Gloucester Cathedral but there was also a third element in which John played a major role. The restoration and rebuilding of the organ was a considerable undertaking which cost John much anxiety and sleepless nights during its execution.

As assistant organist John had been aware of the shortcomings of the seventeenth-century Thomas Harris/Willis organ which had been enlarged and altered during the nineteenth and twentieth centuries and he was determined to overhaul it completely at a time when it needed restoration and repair. Very soon he commissioned Ralph Downes, who had built the Festival Hall organ, to do the work, unaware of the hostility it would cause. The 1666 Thomas Harris organ with its inflated Romantic attachments had many devotees. Many of those familiar with the Gloucester organ were outraged and the public protest disconcerted John for some time. Prominent names like Herbert Howells and John's former teacher, John Dykes Bower, led the protest with such vigour that Ralph Downes attempted to resign from the job two or three times. John became aware of the difficult situation in which he had placed himself and pleaded with Downes to continue with the work, which was carried out by the firm of Hill, Norman and Beard. The opposition rose to a crescendo when the heavier pedal stop, the Double Open 32 foot Wood Pipe was removed because it was not compatible with the bright classical tonal scheme which John envisaged. But in this matter he had the ready support of Seiriol Evans, the Dean, who had long wanted to be rid of it, partly because the sound it made was 'felt rather than heard'.

The full story of the rebuilding of the organ is available elsewhere but in the end it proved to be a great triumph. The instrument was dramatically slimmed down both tonally and structurally and completely rebuilt to a more 'classical' continental tonal scheme. Downes removed some of the nineteenth- and twentieth-century stops and retrieved some of the baroque tone of the original Harris specification, restoring to speech the surviving Harris pipework which had been silent for some eighty years. As Bill Armiger wrote, 'the wonderfully snarling French style reeds, the purer lighter timbre of the foundation stops and the unfamiliar sparkling sonority of the upper-work was surprising to the ears of recital audiences'.[5] John himself was at first rather defensive about the new organ but remained firmly convinced that he had done the right thing and it, of course, reflected the choral style which he introduced into the cathedral. As Mark Blatchly observed, 'Its bright, clear and unfettered speech will continue to remind us of John's choir and his visionary and determined leadership.'

Mark Blatchly also paid a special tribute to the quality of Gloucester's performance when still Organ Scholar of Christ Church, Oxford:

> I was unable to identify a mystery choir on Radio Three Choral Evensong. A rich back row was complemented by a

remarkable treble line, the likes of which I had never heard. It was a thrilling free tone, by turns haunting and brilliant. This it transpired was the work of Sanders of Gloucester. It was shortly to be my privilege to assist in this glorious worship and to discover that the motive force behind the music was a calm, kindly but nonetheless awe-inspiring figure, fond of colourful bow-ties and of a Russian hat – a man to whom fuss of any sort was anathema.

It is said that in any person's career there comes a crisis which will make or break you. The rebuilding of the organ was one such drama for John but it revealed his strong determination, courage and ability to 'see a thing though until it be thoroughly finished which yields the true victory'. And eventually all came to agree that the Gloucester organ is one of the best baroque sounding instruments in the country. Writing in the *Friends of Cathedral Music* magazine, Roger Tucker wrote on hearing the first recital on the organ:

> Organists always do demonstrations well but this was different. We were transported; we had never heard an English organ that sounded so distinctively refined. The player sits at the detached console, facing the south flank of the main case and has the wonderful experience of being able to hear the sound of the organ bouncing back from the nave on his left, while on the right, it is reflected from the huge Crecy window which, because of its slightly bowed shape, gives a sensational sound perspective.[6]

In Gloucester too, as elsewhere, all were aware of John's painstaking organisational competence and meticulous administration. He liked to describe the choir as 'being on parade'. As Mark Blatchly noted, 'there was nothing perfunctory about his tireless captaincy "day by day" throughout the long choir terms of the Church year and his maintenance of high standards'. Yet it was accompanied by an amiable and unthreatening approach such as in the rehearsal of Fauré's *Requiem* when 'he would invariably enjoin the choir at the *Tremens* to "get a bit of fear into it" with a grimace which alarmed some of the younger boys but delighted the Gentlemen who had been expecting it. Such comments did add drama to the rendering and we all knew what was wanted.'

Extra-curricular Activity

Cathedral organists are looked upon as leaders of the ecclesiastical musical tradition in each diocese and an important part of John's work was to encourage parish organists who often ploughed a rather lonely furrow in meeting the challenge of maintaining a choir and persuading the vicar to take an interest in music beyond the menial duty of choosing hymns which were singable. One particular instance of his support and encouragement was his composition of an organ *Soliloquy* (1971) for Cecil Adams, a long-standing organist of Dursley Parish Church. When he reached the senior positions of the Organists' Association he found more than once that he had to defend cathedral music against Deans and Chapters who were less than enthusiastic about the music tradition. On one occasion, at a conference of Deans, Precentors and Organists, one Dean asserted that the music was no more important than the catering or the tourism while it cost a great deal more.

John was an active member of the Organists' Association, being President at one time and a regular spokesman on behalf of the boy choristers. He was also an examiner for the ARCO and FRCO at the Royal College of Organists. At one stage he was an examiner for the Associated Board but eventually resigned.

According to his son, Jonathan, he could not bear to fail people, especially those around middle age who had worked so long and hard with considerable effort to reach the next grade of their ambitions.

John was on the whole reticent about recording the music of Gloucester Cathedral for publication and the discs and CDs which were published numbered rather fewer than other cathedrals. He was always aware of the demands made on the choir and was careful not to allow any extra activity to interfere with the high standards of the daily services. At first he resisted the growing enthusiasm for overseas tours, although by the 1980s he proved to be a full convert, especially enjoying tours to the United States, where enthusiasm for English choral music was boundless.

Before the first tour of the States there had been only one foreign tour to the South of France which, by all accounts, was a low-budget trip. The music was received with considerable enthusiasm in a country which had been starved of good choral singing, especially church music, since the Revolution. Another excursion to France was a brief half-term visit to Dinard in Northern Brittany where the choir sang Mass for Toussaint (All Saints) in St Malo Cathedral for a congregation of well over a thousand and at which Cardinal Gouyon, Archbishop of Rennes, was the celebrant. Concerts were also given in Dol Cathedral and at St Brieuc where the mayor held a reception for the choir. John won the hearts of all present with an inimitable speech in French, attempting to explain the intricacies of Anglican Church music to a bemused audience. Another packed audience heard a very fine concert in St Bartholomew's Anglican Church, Dinard, memorable for an outstanding treble solo from Alex Lewis who became the darling of the French matrons with Mendelssohn's *O for the Wings of a Dove*. The whole choir stayed in a warm, hospitable monastery, the Monastere St Francois, where another more informal concert was given as well as another Mass in the context of an Ecumenical service at which all were able to receive Holy Communion. On such occasions John was in his sociable element while retaining a strict control of the choir's performance. One musical initiative by a group of choristers, led by Ben Moxon and Philip Webb, which did not entirely meet with John's approval, was an impromptu Barber's Shop close harmony group which entertained passengers in the various lounges of the Brittany Ferry during the crossing in order to supplement their pocket money.

Perhaps the most memorable tour was the second visit to the United States. The first trip in 1989 lasted for just a week, beginning with a concert in Gloucester, Massachusetts and continuing with five other concerts and three services in the beautiful New England area when the cherry blossoms were all out, and ending up in Washington, DC 'which was of course completely crackers'. For the next one in 1991, John's gift of meticulous preparation was supremely apparent and appreciated by all involved.

During the year before the tour, and largely unknown to anyone but a few, John went round Gloucester and sought sponsorship from supporters, including Walls Ice Cream factory, to cover the £27,000 cost of the venture. He also went off to the States by himself to liaise with the host cities, not only to organise the services and concerts which were being planned but also to arrange outings and attractive venues for relaxation. No detail was overlooked and the clockwork arrangements covered every eventuality. John remained very much in control throughout the trip. It is perhaps appropriate to record an article written soon after the return by Mark Blatchly, for *Choir Schools Today*.

On US Air flight 1 181 the choristers soon won over the affec-
tions of the flight attendants who requested them to gather
in the tail of the aeroplane to sing *God Save the Queen* over
the PA system. Thus the first public performance was neither
scheduled (we soon learned to pronounce it 'skeduled') nor
sanctioned by John Sanders. On arrival we knew we were in
the deep South when the main item for sale in the airport
buffet was a local delicacy, 'sawl dawg'.

Our tour really began when we arrived at St Philip's Cathedral, Atlanta, at the precise time planned by John Sanders to
meet our first hosts. His meticulous organisation and planning involving so many people was characteristic of the
whole trip and is an abiding memory. Relaxed American
hospitality and generosity ensured that we all met next
morning full of expectation but largely unprepared for the
quite overwhelming Cyclorama painting of the Civil War
battle of Atlanta and the extravaganza of the World of Coke
with its larger than life advertising, the brilliant tap-room
representation (where John was called a 'jerk' by the barman
for daring to suggest that the original Coca Cola was generously endowed with cocaine!) and abundant soft drinks
supplied in a psychedelic high-tech environment.

At lunch we experienced the first of the lunches at Morri-
son's café. Our pre-paid vouchers, organised by John,
allowed seven dishes of truly gargantuan proportions from
shrimps and other salads (a meal in itself), a galaxy of
assorted fresh fruit, a variety of entrees, cooked vegetables,
gateaux laden with cream and chocolate, a variety of rolls and
the inevitable liberally iced drinks. The sight of the choristers
staggering along with their mountainous trays of food led
anxious minds to ponder the recovery time from such a
meal. For there was serious work to do.

Americans are familiar with good church music and are at
least as discerning as their English counterparts. St Philip's
Cathedral has a mixed choir, the boys 'St David's' choir and

the girls 'St Cecilia's' choir with excellent facilities for practice, a pattern reflected in the other cathedrals and churches
we visited. A good proportion of the capacity audience knew
what to expect from an English cathedral choir and were
particularly expectant as the Cathedral had just completed a
major project of tiling the underside of the roof to improve
the acoustics. At the end of the final item, John Sanders'
Easter Carol with its splendidly appropriate musical accla-
mation of resurrection faith, the audience rose in a
spontaneous standing ovation. They loved the choir and the
sheer tingling beauty of the music. At the reception afterwards it was rather humbling to know that we were being
lavishly entertained by the same church members who were
providing soup kitchen meals in the undercroft for some
1500 destitute and homeless people each week.

Next day wise adults went on a shopping expedition while
the choristers ran amok among the hands-on exhibits at the
Sci-Track museum before going on to the historic town of
Macon. On the way they were able to release their energies
amongst the broad acres of America's oldest historic site, the
Indian settlement at Oemulgee. In the evening another
capacity crowd came to hear the first performance in Christ
Church by an English cathedral choir. There was another
prolonged standing ovation and afterwards the rector and Dr
Richard Nelson, organist, both declared that their aim was to
have an English choir every year.

Charleston was pure magic. Here is a city, dating from the
first British Empire, which is intent on preserving its heritage
and its beauty. Our demure guide, wearing a little straw hat
with cream matching gloves, who showed us round on a
lightning tour, could herself have stepped from the pages of
Louisa M. Alcott. St Philip's Episcopal Church is strongly
charismatic and revivalist but nevertheless fully aware of the
spiritual worth of excellent music. The crowded church
appreciated in particular Benjamin Britten's *Missa Brevis*

sung by the choristers and Mark Lee's organ solo *Variations and Fugue on God Save the King* by Max Reger. The choir enjoyed another standing ovation.

Savannah is also proud of its British origin and the influence of the engineer officer Major Oglethorpe pervades the town. Proud too is St John's Episcopal Church of its role as the centre of the American Prayer Book Society. The carefully prepared programme by John, complete with words, was ruthlessly changed from contemporary language into the language of the King James Bible and the Book of Common Prayer. Even Richard Shepherd's *Gloria*, recently composed for the new Rita A Holy Communion Service, was resolutely printed with the old words. Savannah was memorable for the welcome received, the privilege of dining in an historic home, now part of the church complex, which General Sherman used as his headquarters during the Civil War, the azaleas in the magnificent square and the riverside market stalls.

But we had to leave the old Deep South for the vibrant new Florida and Jacksonville, to which a large part of the US Gulf Fleet had just returned. After the Eucharist in the chapel at the Naval base on the Sunday morning, the commandant's wife stood up and exhorted everyone to attend the concert by Gloucester Cathedral choir at St Paul's-by-the-sea that afternoon. No doubt that helped to produce another crowded church on a bright, sunny afternoon when the lure of the beach must have been strong even for locals accustomed to such weather. This was the outstanding concert of the tour. Everything was right for it; an ultra modern, high walled church shaped like a fish provided a perfect acoustic, an immaculate organ and the choir at the top of its form. Everyone emerged into the bright sunlight the better for the experience. The atmosphere was possibly best expressed by the woman in tears who left early, giving Richard Gambold, our tour manager, a cheque for $100 and telling him it was the most moving experience of her life.

And so to Orlando, Disney World, surely the choristers' paradise, and the Kennedy Space Centre at Cape Canaveral where the exotic wildlife competes on equal terms with the technology. St Luke's Cathedral has a very good choir recently made famous by appearing in a TV commercial for Disney World. They have sung in King's College Chapel, Cambridge and other centres of musical excellence in England. The congregation is discerning and knowledgeable. The choir, which should by now have been exhausted, surpassed themselves and after a magnificent second half, responded to the standing ovation with an encore, *I was Glad*, which sent the audience wild. Typically of John Sanders, in the midst of the emotional triumph of the occasion at the end of a brilliant but demanding tour, he did not forget that the occasion marked Robert Armiger's finale of his career as a chorister and marked the occasion with a special mention that the choice of encore was made by Robert.[7]

The cathedral choristers in New York – the twin towers in the background

By this time in 1991 John Sanders had developed a taste for overseas tours and was to complete another one of Canada and New York district before he retired. The same attention to detail, the same thoughtful choice of programme, the same courteous thoughtfulness and gratitude toward his hosts brought the same adulation and appreciation. No wonder his music has been selling so well in that continent where many choirs are performing it.

The Choral Society

It was in the Choral Society that John's personality and manner became a legend. Within a strictly disciplined routine, the door of the Chapter House where the choir practised was locked five minutes after the start. Failure to attend seventy-five per cent of rehearsals meant that you could not take part in the concert. Yet there was a lightness and wholeheartedness which encouraged everyone to enjoy each Monday evening. He was a brilliant choral director and, as Roger Tucker wrote, 'there was an aura of great strength which commanded respect and inspired everyone to give more than they thought themselves capable of'. During his years there was an astonishing variety of works sung over a quarter of a century of music making. Handel, Mozart, Bach's *Passions* and *B Minor Mass*, Berlioz's *Grand Mass*, Finzi, Howells' *Hymnus Paradisi*, Elgar's *Dream of Gerontius*, on one occasion with the CBSO, *Caractacus*, *The Apostles*, *The Kingdom*, Rossini's *Petite Messe Solonnelle*, Fauré and Duruflé, together with many other shorter works became part of the society's repertoire. One particularly difficult work, remembered well by all who sang it, was the African *Sanctus*. Second basses recall it for the requirement to reach a top F sharp from time to time. The accompaniment was being played by a specialist virtuoso group which was already heavily committed to a concert programme in London, and so it had to be relayed to Gloucester electronically. John thus had to don headphones and use a stopwatch thus, as one tenor put it, 'looking like a spitfire pilot'. It was John's belief and intention that a choir should always have something new to work on and to look forward to. He himself prepared each piece of music with meticulous care which was apparent from the first rehearsal.

John could create a feeling of excitement during the toughest period of practice although he would not tolerate any casual singing. Of course the first encounter with the Choral Society, as with the cathedral choir, was the audition, again in the family house in Miller's Green. John himself recounted the number of gifts that were received as aspirants came for their audition. Eggs, a chicken, baskets of vegetables and the occasional bottle of wine were amongst offerings received but it was not all one way. My wife Frances turned up in such a state of nerves that she was given a large tumbler of gin and tonic before being ushered into the practice room. Once again Janet was the unfailingly reassuring presence with her ready smile and matter-of-fact manner which everyone loved and admired.

There were some memorable auditions. As he was about to retire John recalled the woman who was invited to sight-read a piece of music, a requirement of every applicant. When she was half-way through the passage, John stopped her and said, 'Your sight-reading is not too bad but you are neglecting the rhythm.' 'Sod the rhythm,' was the retort, 'I'm having enough difficulty finding the notes.' She was successful and ever after she was known as 'Sod the rhythm'.

Gloucester Choral Society

Once in the choir there was no relaxation or resting on laurels. One always felt that there was room for improvement and sometimes the demands for perfection seemed to be unobtainable. This was admirably expressed by Joan Sadler, former headmistress of Cheltenham Ladies' College, who admitted to feeling rather like the dairy cows that were standing at a gate watching the traffic pass by. They saw an enormous milk lorry with a slogan on the side: 'Our milk is sterilised, pasteurised and homogenised with added calcium.' One cow said to her neighbour, 'Do you ever get the feeling that we are totally inadequate?' This was a fairly common feeling within the choir, especially on those 'rare and terrible moments' when John would alight from his podium and walk up and down the rows in search of careless intonation. 'I can hear a warble,' would be the ominous, lugubrious prelude to the perambulation.

Yet amidst the tension and effort there was never a hint of

sarcasm or any remark which might humiliate. In a radio tribute one lady summed up the atmosphere: 'John Sanders took great pains never to embarrass anyone and was always so thoroughly courteous and fair-minded.'

People began to look forward to his droll remarks and dry comments during rehearsal and Mark Blatchly, his assistant organist, became almost convinced that John held a script meeting before rehearsals: 'His remarks often had double meaning, some of them so intricate and finely-wrought, that they could not have been entirely spontaneous.' He remembers a Monday evening in February when, mildly exasperated by some weary singing, John turned to his left and, aping the dreary delivery of the chorus, said, 'What's the matter sopranos? Hasn't anyone sent you a Valentine card?' When order was restored the choral singing was transformed.

At his retirement party several people recalled moments when John's dry humour, always apparently spontaneous and without any hint of double meaning, caused instant laughter: 'Ladies, you are responsible for the pool of Siloam'; 'Tenors, you sound like tearing calico'; 'The basses are singing down a drainpipe'; 'Tenors, come off the clouds quick!'; 'Ladies, you are being slightly pulled in by the gentlemen'; 'Contraltos, you are doing it far too voluptuously'; 'Tenors, you are singing the D sharp on the loo' (of Alleluia!). After each remark which caused a ripple of laughter, John would look up surprised and say, 'Have I said something?', which would cause even more merriment. Perhaps the young lady was right when discussing John's charisma on the radio: 'He had a gift of saying the wrong thing at the right time', and she quoted him during a rehearsal for a concert in which the theme was 'Making love, not war' – 'Ladies, make love with me in my time, not yours.'[8]

Tributes also came from visitors. Professional orchestras who occasionally came to play with the Choral Society were unanimous in acknowledging the immensely careful preparation John had made over the music as well as his tactful, yet commanding leadership. 'He had an unusual gift of bridging the gap between amateurs and professionals,' remarked one member of the Gloucestershire Symphony Orchestra, which John regularly conducted. And one experienced visiting soloist of international reputation said of him, 'He is way out and above the rest of the people I have worked with. There is a touch of grace about him.'

Audiences too invariably showed very great appreciation of his masterly conducting and on at least two occasions, one after the oratorio *Samson*, he was given a standing ovation – a rare occurence in Britain.

Perhaps the last word should again be given to Mark Blatchly who worked so closely with John in cathedral choir and Choral Society for so many years: 'He gave us all, singers and players, confidence. His encouraging direction played to his performers' strengths allowing them comfortable elbow room within the carefully planned Sanders interpretation. He inculcated a rare blend of concentration and relaxation. We all did our best for him because we wanted to, we thought he was terrific. He also made us laugh.'

John also took control of the newly constituted Gloucestershire Symphony Orchestra which he conducted for some twenty-seven years with the same meticulous dedication. One member of the orchestra commented on his great ability to treat amateur and professional musicians with equal courtesy and care.

The Campaign for the Traditional Cathedral Choir (CTCC)

Towards the end of his working life, John became more and more concerned about the future of the English choral tradition which has owed so much to the regular excellence and leadership of the cathedrals throughout the country. In spite of being Director of Music at one of the most famous girls' schools in the country, he began to fear for the traditional boys' choir for whom most serious church music had been written. In the TV programme on the King's School and choristers, this question was raised by the production team, particularly as the girls had recently joined the Upper School for the first time. During these years of the 1980s there was no trouble in attracting boy applicants for treble places and, although girls' choirs were being experimented with in other parts of the country, there was no question of allowing girls to be part of the cathedral choir in Gloucester.[9]

This caused some discussion amongst the young girls interviewed on the programme. Juliet Groves, at the age of twelve, was one of the leading proponents of girl choristers, strongly supported by the formidable Jessica Chamberlayne. While she was still in the Junior School and before the decision had been made to allow the girls to stay on in the Senior School, Jessica had written to the headmaster demanding that she should be considered for entry to the Upper School. Although she risked being the only girl in her year, her confident assertion of female rights overcame the timid male opposition and she won her case. Still only thirteen, she made a powerful case for girl choristers during the television programme: 'I sometimes sing solos in the cathedral with the school choir and they tell me I sing like a boy. I think girls ought to have the chance to be in the choir for they get free education while the girls are excluded and have to pay fees!' Not all the girls agreed and Julia Bowland, amongst others, was heard to say that the cathedral tradition was an ancient and important one and should not be interfered with. Philip Webb, the Head Chorister, was firm in his belief that boys' and girls' voices do not blend at that age and that the long tradition of boy choristers had made them more adapted to the demanding nature of the large cathedral acoustics.

In the same programme John Sanders said that although girls were now singing in some cathedral choirs, they were usually found in cathedrals that were formerly parish churches where perhaps they found it difficult to recruit boys and that in Gloucester it would be quite a time before girls would become Foundation choristers. He also appealed to the Statutes of Henry VIII where it was stated that 'there shall be at least twelve choristers and six probationers who shall be boys who are baptised' along with other children whom the headmaster shall select. This distinction between 'boys' and 'children' enabled the King's School to go co-educational after 450 years without having to go to the Privy Council to alter the statutes. John and I were both relieved to find that King Henry had stated a form of words which still fulfilled the requirements of a cathedral and school in the late twentieth and early twenty-first century.

Soon after the inauguration of the campaign, John very willingly agreed to become president and was an active participant. For him it was more than the wish to preserve a tradition which had gone on for more than a thousand years, although he was no musical misogynist. He was for instance supportive of women priests when they were finally ordained and that male tradition had lasted for a good deal longer. He was quite seriously doubtful about the nature of the young female voice, compared with a boy's. His experience in a very large acoustic setting of a cathedral with a special resonance like Gloucester's had led him to believe that a mature boy's voice had within it not only a clarity and purity of tone, but also an urgency and intensity which no girl could capture. He was fond of saying that superb choral singing and solo work 'is the only thing that a little boy can do better than anyone else'. He was also aware that the choristers loved singing music that reached very high notes, even top C, and they were proud of being able to reach them without apparent effort. He put down the difference in quality at this age to the fact that boys know that they can only sing this top-line range for a few years, from eight to thirteen or fourteen, while girls knew they would be singing the top line from eight to eighty!

Another important reason for the preservation of the professionally trained boys' choir was John's concern for the future of the lower parts. During a discussion I had with him he asked the question, 'If we lose the boy trebles who are trained to such a high degree of sight-reading and musicianship, where are we going to find the adequately qualified men to fulfil their duties in the lower parts?'

Of course he was quite aware of the collapse of the church male choirs. During the late 1950s, when he began his work as an assistant, there were about 190,000 boys singing in parish church choirs. By 2005, the year after John's death, there were 700. At the same time there was a sharp rise in the number of girls from virtually zero to more than 80,000. But by the turn of the millennium the number of girl choristers was falling fast which has left the church in the sad situation that neither boys nor girls are finding their way into regular singing choirs.

The reasons for the decline in boy choristers have been

much debated and there are varying degrees of prejudice shown by all interested parties. The point has been made that private Preparatory Schools and Independent Schools still produce choirs of high quality for liturgical worship and secular concerts while very few boys are singing in the maintained schools. Dr Saunders, in an article in the CTCC's magazine argues that part of this problem arises from the total feminisation of the infant and primary schools. Boys no longer have any male role models to follow and are likely to feel alienated from what has now become an activity for the girls. The evidence is that this may be an accurate reflection of what is happening, for girls far outnumber boys in school choirs, which are often wholly female.

John realised that the danger of such an organisation as the campaign could easily be confused with a sexist reaction to the prevailing feminism which is often quite eager to seize upon anything which challenges the role of women. John distanced himself from any such notion. After all he was a successful Director of Music at Cheltenham Ladies' College and was fully aware of the excellence of the singing and musicianship shown by girls. His support was entirely due to his concern for the maintenance of the Anglican cathedral tradition. He was worried that the development of mixed choirs or two separate cathedral choirs would water down the commitment and support which they enjoy at the moment.

He may be proved right. One of my grandsons was a cathedral chorister at a time when there was only one choir and the boys rehearsed ten or eleven times, mornings and evenings, each week as well as singing six public services. With the Three Choirs Festival interrupting the summer holidays and Christmas and Easter making their demands during the other school holidays, membership of the choir became a definite way of life with all the discipline, professionalism and commitment it involved. His younger brother is now a chorister alongside a separate girls' choir. Although the boys sing more often than the girls, they do have a lot more free time than formerly, including two weekends a month. While it is difficult to assess the resulting quality of performance there is no doubt that he is far less involved and committed than his older brother. Neither does he seem so concerned to produce an excellent performance.

Chapter Six

The Three Choirs Festival and the Williamson Affair

Ever since the beginning of the seventeenth century, organists of the cathedrals of Gloucester, Hereford and Worcester have been responsible for bringing the three choirs together and for arranging artists to perform the music. The Three Choirs Festival claims to be the oldest continuing music festival in the world and it is certainly the most famous choral festival, attracting in the twentieth century people from every part of the world.

Although 1717 or thereabouts seems to be the accepted date of the beginning of the regular meetings of the choirs, there is circumstantial evidence, as mentioned previously, that some sort of celebratory gathering was held at the Restoration some fifty-five years before. Anthony Boden records a 'legend' known by Elgar and Sir Ivor Atkins which relates a meeting of the Gloucester and Worcester choirs in Worcester in 1662. This is entirely feasible as there were strong connections between the two cities, notably with the Tomkins family, the most famous of whom, Thomas, was the composer and organist of Worcester before the civil war and, as a boy, had been a chorister in Gloucester. The political situation also made it advisable for the Roundhead Gloucester men to join the Royalist Worcester citizens to celebrate the repair to the fabric and organ after the destruction caused by the Parliamentary army. This would be a signal to the deeply suspicious King Charles II that Gloucester folk had realised the error of their ways and were anxious to display their loyalty to the Crown. As a young prince Charles had witnessed the failure of the Royalist forces to overcome Gloucester's defences.

Be that as it may, the meeting of the Three Choirs had become an established event each year from early in the eighteenth century and by 1724 there seems to have been an amalgamation of informal religious and secular Musick Meetings along with the establishment of a charity 'for assisting the education and maintenance of the orphans of the poorer clergy belonging to the dioceses of Gloucester, Worcester and Hereford'.[1] This had been pressed for by Dr Thomas Bisse, brother of Philip Bisse who had been President of the Corporation of the Sons of the Clergy in London from 1717–21. The Three Choirs charity continued until the late 1980s when it was decided that clergy orphans and widows were well-provided for by other means.

During this early period of the meeting of the Three Choirs, the timing of it was often planned to coincide with the horse races, the completion of the harvest and autumn season balls for the gentry. It was not unknown for other choirs and musicians to join the three cathedral choirs for, as Anthony Boden quotes from the *Gloucester Journal* of 29th August 1745:

> This day, Dr Greene, Master of his Majesty's Band of Musick, with several gentlemen belonging to the Chapel Royal, Westminster Abbey and St Paul's, set out for Gloucester, where they are to meet the Gentlemen belonging to the Choirs of Worcester, Hereford and Gloucester in order to perform on Wednesday and Thursday next, a Grand Concert of Musick,

both vocal and instrumental, for the benefit of poor Clergy-men's widows and their children.[2]

Dr Greene was a fairly prolific composer of dignified church music but little of his work is sung today apart from the harvest anthem *Thou Visitest the Earth*.

One striking characteristic of the Three Choirs Festival during these early years was the speed with which new music was adopted into the repertoire. Handel's music was being performed as early as 1736, when his *Te Deum* was sung in Gloucester and thereafter, Handel became a staple diet of the Festival for the next two centuries. According to Anthony Boden, the *Messiah* was sung at every festival but two from 1757 to 1963. There was however a tradition, even from early days, to introduce and encourage new music. This became an important feature of the Festival alongside the hardy annuals such as Mendelssohn's *Elijah* in the nineteenth century and Elgar's *Dream of Gerontius* in the twentieth.

When John entered into this long tradition of musical excellence, the days of Elgar's and Vaughan Williams' presence at the Festival were over and the time had come for a new look at the organisation and repertoire. New organists such as Christopher Robinson of Worcester and Richard Lloyd of Hereford were busy introducing modern works from Michael Tippett, Alan Hoddinott and others as well as still attracting the best-known soloists, but there were signs of unease about the future of the Festival. Writing in *The Times* during the 1967 festival, William Mann asked

Is it to be regarded ipso facto as an event of national cultural importance, to be judged by the standards of, say, Glyndebourne or Edinburgh? Or as a shop window for all that is most worth while in choral and orchestral music of all countries and periods? Or do we have to admit that an existence of 240 years inevitably induces some sort of senile decay and that, in its present form, the Three Choirs Festival needs to be retired or replaced for the musical health of the country?

This was indeed a challenge to the three Musical Directors and Festival Committees. However, as John knew from the first, they had some great strengths which other musical gatherings lacked. By the time he came on to the scene there was very wide support from all over the world, especially from the United States, which meant that stewardships and general tickets sold out very quickly. A special atmosphere had grown up around the Festival Club which attracted old friends and musicians year after year. In particular music teachers, especially those involved in school choirs and choral societies, were attracted to a festival which made choral music a central attraction. During the Festival they could meet and compare notes, discover new music and share their experiences. Attendees such as Dr Frederick Bacon-Shone from California were annual visitors.

Another strength, which John was passionate about, was the local atmosphere of the Festival. While the leading orchestras and soloists came from elsewhere, the chorus was entirely local, with the 'home team' producing the bulk of the choir each year and the three organists having the lion's share of conducting the various works, even the instrumental ones. No other major festival depends so much on local administration and talent and this creates a strong 'parochial' atmosphere and welcome. Everyone is made to feel at home and is aware of meeting up with two or three thousand people who share the same musical interests.

On the other hand, if it was to remain a genuinely international festival, there was a need to have an internationally known 'father figure' associated with it. As we have seen this had been provided by Sir Edward Elgar and Vaughan Williams in the immediate past. John had felt they were 'looking over his shoulder', but the latter had died in 1958. Herbert Howells was also a regular visitor to the Festival in all three cathedrals but 'he was getting to be a very old man by then, so we didn't involve him very much'. During his time John encouraged Sir Charles Groves to replace Sir Adrian Boult and he conducted Parry's *Symphonic Variations* at John's first Festival. At one time there was an effort to persuade Benjamin Britten to become involved but, as John remarked with some regret, 'he didn't take any interest in it'. More recently there has been a tendency to invite well-known personalities to conduct. Towards the end of his life John became hostile to this trend for he feared that it would damage the essential local nature of the Festival.

John's principle in choosing works for performance is expressed in a letter he wrote to Miss Heather Swanston, a student at Bath who was writing a dissertation on the Three Choirs Festival for her BA degree. She was asking if John thought the Festival was still fulfilling the role it had in the past and whether it had contributed anything to English music. His reply in September 1977 is noteworthy because he made clear that he had a very positive and optimistic view of the continuing importance of the Festival, in spite of some previously lukewarm and even hostile press comments:

a) When commissioning a new work for the Festival one obviously wants to choose a composer who is going to be sympathetic to the Festival audience and also to the ability of the chorus. We try to strike a balance between commissioning works from young, up and coming composers and those already established.

b) The Festivals have always made an enormous contribution to promoting English music. Had it not been for the Three Choirs Festival very few modern English choral works would have seen the light of day! Our Festival is one of the only musical organisations commissioning new choral music.

c) In the past the Festival tended to concentrate on a few composers e.g. Handel 17th century, Elgar at the end of the 19th century, and Vaughan Williams very recently. Nowadays it is our policy to make the programme more representative of the international music scene.

d) Judging from this year's results, I foresee a very bright future for the Festival. The demand for tickets was greater than ever before and the Festival received very favourable notices in the press. I am sure it will go on discharging its responsibility for bringing forward new English Choral Music and also presenting the best music of all periods and nationalities.[3]

Another consideration in the selection of music, which was omitted in John's letter to Miss Swanston, but was regularly observed, was the celebration of anniversaries of composers and musicians. This was evident at the first Festival for which John was responsible in 1968 when Rossini's *Stabat Mater* was performed, commemorating the centenary of the composer's death. A first performance of Christopher Steel's *Mass* was also performed, conducted by John.

Evident at this Festival was a situation which was to plague the Musical Director continually. Orchestras and soloists had to be booked well in advance and from time to time they found themselves unable to carry out their commitments. On this occasion Rita Streich, the first foreign singer to appear for many years, had to call off at the last minute on account of illness. John was told of this two days before the opening service and a replacement had to be found. The agent suggested Richard Lewis who was currently singing in Tel Aviv. He flew from Israel on the Tuesday, sang in the broadcast concert on the Thursday, then immediately left to sing at the Edinburgh Festival the following day. At this Festival Sir Adrian Boult was the guest conductor who conducted Sir Hubert Parry's *Symphony Variations*, commemorating the composer's death fifty years before.[4]

Friends of John and Janet, who came to the Worcester Festival from Chester in 1969, recall being amongst the first audience to clap a performance in the cathedral. This had been discouraged and even deplored in previous years. The occasion was a performance by the National Youth Orchestra when it must have been felt that the young players deserved recognition. Later in the week Peter Maxwell's *Five Carols for Boys' Voices* was applauded but on the next day Rossini's effervescent *Petite Messe Solennelle* was greeted by a 'strange silence'. At a broadcast concert later in the week, Sir Adrian Boult, conducting the Royal Philharmonic Orchestra, made a point of requesting that there should be no applause. Today it seems odd that there should have ever been a time when applause in church was disapproved of but up to the 1970s it was a cause of considerable disquiet. The modern habit of giving a rousing cheer or yelp coinciding with the last chord of music seems to be a complete violation of appreciation and is to be thoroughly deplored. Many conductors including John have developed a way of holding the last beat so that the few moments' silence can complete the work. In his later years John became more and more concerned that the music he produced should be surrounded by silence.

John's first real effort at commissioning a new work came

in 1971 when Alan Hoddinott was invited to compose a work called *The Tree of Life*. It was a foretaste of things to come for John observed afterwards what a 'dicey business commissioning is because you never know what you are going to get or whether it's going to be finished'. In Hoddinott's case, he had already failed to complete a work commissioned for the Hereford Festival in 1970. John must have become increasingly worried about the chances of obtaining the full score in time, for the composer would drive up from Cardiff at about 8 o'clock on a Sunday morning with about ten sheets of manuscript which he had just finished, and when things were getting a bit desperate would 'add a bottle of champagne just to keep things sweet'. Later John did say that the advantage of the regular Three Choirs Festival is that 'deserving works' can be repeated in succeeding years when the first performance might have been dodgy. This was the case with such works as the Williamson *Mass of Christ the King* and Gerard Schurmann's *Piers Plowman*.

It was at the opening service of this Festival that John's great undertaking on his arrival in Gloucester was completed with the re-dedication of the cathedral organ. It attracted much attention and a special organ concerto by Peter Dickinson was performed to celebrate the occasion. Later in the week the Prime Minister, Edward Heath, attended the Festival and, being a former organ scholar, was invited to try the restored organ out for himself.

When Roy Massey arrived in Hereford in 1974, he admits to being somewhat awed by the number of first-class orchestras and musicians he would have to find to fill a Three Choirs programme. 'How and where do you get them from?' he asked John Sanders. Roy remembers being advised that it would be a good idea to have a meeting of the Three Choirs Committee in the October before the Festival! It soon

Edward Heath, Prime Minister, playing the newly restored organ

became clear that preparations for the next 'home' Festival had to begin as soon as the last one was over. Orchestras and soloists had to be booked up to three years in advance and the programme had to be produced for publication the year before. There was a considerable amount of hard thinking and stress involved to assemble an undertaking which demanded more and more time in addition to the daily round of services and teaching. It was necessary for the three cathedral organists to meet regularly to exchange ideas and information and this was not always easy in view of the demands on their time. It was remarkable how the triumvirate of John Sanders, Roy Massey and Donald Hunt adapted to the particular stresses of the task and were able to remain calm and apparently unfazed when everyone else was staggering from crisis to crisis. While other great Festivals were increasingly moving toward a full-time professional organisation, the bulk of the Three Choirs work was done by amateur supporters, with each cathedral city and community taking the responsibility in turn. But the mainstay had to be the cathedral organist.

Gloucester 1977 – The Williamson Affair[5]

1977 was a special year in the life of Gloucester Cathedral, the Three Choirs Festival and of John Sanders who, as the local director, was responsible for organising and arranging the music and the performers. Not only was it the Queen's Silver Jubilee but by the generally accepted reckoning it commemorated the 250th meeting of the Three Choirs.

Anthony Boden in his excellent history of the Festival records six orchestras, thirty soloists, seven conductors and a number of instrumental and choral groups from the Commonwealth who came together for an event lasting eight days from 20th to 28th August. Incidentally, one of the choral groups, the Dorian Singers, came from New Zealand, directed by Peter Godfrey, former chorister and choral scholar at King's College Chapel, Cambridge who, as we have seen, had been invited to become organist and director of music at Gloucester Cathedral on the retirement of Herbert Sumsion.

For this Festival new works were commissioned from Harrison Birtwistle, Peter Maxwell Davies, Rory Boyle, Ronald Tremain and Tony Hewitt-Jones with the centrepiece being a *Mass of Christ the King* by Malcolm Williamson, Master of the Queen's Musick and dedicated to Her Majesty for her Jubilee.

With an ambitious programme aimed at featuring the music of composers who had had a major influence on the Festival there were bound to be some uncertainties and disappointments. One early and major one was the exclusion of Richard Rodney Bennett's suite, *The Christians*, which was based on music he had written for a television series of the same name. But there were soon hints that the Williamson Mass might also run into difficulties.

Malcolm Williamson was an extraordinary person of great ability and talent for hard work. As well as being a musician, he held doctorates in medicine and psychology and held a university fellowship studying the problems of handicapped children.

Anthony Boden quotes the experience of Paul Jennings, one of the most influential journalists of his day, when he visited Williamson to interview him prior to a performance of his *The Violins of St Jacques* on the radio, which was one of his most successful operas, first performed in 1976. He found that he had been up all night working on the *Mass of Christ the King*. Jennings quotes Williamson:

> 'Messiaen said "Je suis musicien surtout catholique", and that's what I am: I became a Catholic when I was twenty – it was terrible, I can't imagine any other idea of life. Come and look at this. I was struggling with it last night.' On the piano was the *Kyrie* of a *Mass of Christ the King*. 'The feast of Christ the King was created only in modern times. I'm very interested in it: what we need is this gentle authority of God. See: the soprano calls out, higher each time, above the choir *Kyrie Eleison*, have mercy on us – come in, you're in a choir: let's have a go…'

In March 1977, there was a press conference at the Arts Council offices in Piccadilly to announce details of the Gloucester Festival. Williamson, having arrived late, embarked on a bitter attack against the Arts Council for rejecting his application for a £5000 grant to complete the work and for 'the long list of humiliations I have suffered from the Arts Council over a great many years'. He was only able to undertake the work because of a promise of £2000 from the Johnson Wax Company after completion and a loan from the Royal Philharmonic Orchestra.

Consequent news reports highlighted the grievances Williamson expressed at this conference and a number of newspaper articles expressed concern at the pitiful commission fees paid to composers in the country. It was to become a source of irritation and anxiety to John Sanders in later years when he was at last able to turn to more serious composition.

It was soon evident that Williamson had taken on far more work than he had time for. In 1977 he was already committed to an American tour in July and before that, he wrote the music for Richard Adams's *Watership Down*. He was also composing a mini-opera for the Queen's Jubilee to be performed by thousands of schoolchildren in Liverpool and a symphony to be performed by the London Philharmonic Orchestra in London.

One month before the Festival, John Sanders knew that the Mass would not be finished in time. The vocal parts were there, colour-coded in three parts, the last section of which arrived two weeks before the Festival. Orchestral parts were another matter. One week before the Festival John was in London with the Royal Philharmonic Orchestra for an orchestral rehearsal when, half-way through, Simon Campion, Williamson's assistant, arrived in a taxi with about two-thirds of the orchestrations. From then on bits of the score arrived piecemeal by train each day to Gloucester.

Malcolm Williamson turned up in Gloucester on the very day of the performance with a few more missing parts and feverishly tried to complete the orchestration by adding additional parts during a hastily arranged last-minute rehearsal. John finally called a halt with the agreement of the Royal Philharmonic Orchestra and the performance went ahead without the *Gloria* and *Credo*. The fully scored responsorial psalm for solo tenor and orchestra was also omitted: although it was now fully scored, it had failed to be submitted by John Sanders' deadline. The *Agnus Dei* was accompanied by the organ. The programme was revised to include Herbert Howells' *Festival Fanfare*, Elgar's arrangement of the National Anthem and Handel's *Zadok the Priest* and *The King Shall Rejoice*.

What is not so well known is that John went to meet Malcolm Williamson in the Festival Office at 7.40 p.m., just before the concert was due to start at 8 p.m. In a letter to Mrs Reader of New South Wales, John wrote.

> He seemed rather put out that I intended to perform the *Agnus Dei* with organ only as the orchestral parts had not been provided. He tried to do a deal with me, saying that if he allowed me to perform the *Agnus Dei*, I should let him conduct the *Psalmus Responsorius*. He had brought the orchestral parts with him on that evening and there had been no possibility of rehearsing it with the orchestra, who had finished their rehearsal at 4 p.m. I told him that it was very doubtful that the orchestra would agree to play it without rehearsal, and pointed out that there could be mistakes in the parts, but I said that I would go and talk to the orchestra to see what they felt. On arrival in the Cathedral cloisters, I found Simon Campion and the orchestra Librarian checking the parts, but they found that the number of bars did not correspond and I therefore said quite definitely that there was no possibility of performing the movement. I then went on to the platform at 8 p.m. and proceeded with the concert.

Unknown to John, Malcolm Williamson caused quite a stir and disturbance at the back of the cathedral and Simon Campion had to restrain him from entering by the slype door. Dr Jim Hoyland and others managed to calm Williamson down after half an hour or so and at the end of the concert he made an appearance on the stage, rather to John's surprise, kissed the lady soloists and shook John by the hand.

Under the stage afterwards he told John that he had never been so insulted in all his life that he had not been allowed to conduct the *Psalmus Responsorius.* One might have thought that would put an end to their brief relationship.

After a report of the incident in the Australian newspapers, Malcolm Williamson threatened to sue for libel, but was persuaded not to pursue this as the British press had not mentioned it and nothing particularly derogatory had been claimed.

In spite of the problems and the occasional outbreaks of artistic emotion the first performance was a considerable success. Looking back on the evening the *Church Times* reported that, 'Sanders had to achieve a viable performance of an incomplete work from an incomplete score, while the composer offered to copy out parts for the unfinished sections on the day, and seriously expected the orchestra and choir to perform from these, sight unseen. Sanders gently vetoed this, and performed what was ready to score.' The verdict was that he had saved the day and with it Williamson's reputation.

Prior to the concert there had been considerable interest in this work dedicated to the Queen and performed at the 250th anniversary of the oldest music festival in the world. It occasioned a renewed interest by the media in the Festival and reviews afterwards were positive. Richard Crichton in the *Financial Times* looked forward to hearing the whole work while William Mann in *The Times* wrote that he could 'only assure those readers who spurn Williamson's simplistic music (its invention all the stronger because it has to be instantly performable) that the new Mass is an elaborate composition, grand and often surprising, for all that the composition draws on ecclesiastical traditions, especially on plainsong. It makes a jubilant and variegated noise, approachable yet demanding concentration.'

At the time it was sad that Williamson failed to appreciate the considerate and characteristically diplomatic way in which John handled the difficult situation. He was upset that he had not been invited to conduct the work himself and had failed to appreciate the pride that John and the Festival Committee took in creating an essentially local festival atmosphere. In correspondence with the editor of the local newspaper, *The Citizen*, he scornfully dismissed the Three Choirs Festival as a 'citadel of amateurism'. Later, when the completed work had been successfully performed, Malcolm Williamson was generous in acknowledging his debt to John.

There was a sequel. Later in the same year Williamson failed to complete his *Symphony No. 4* for a performance by the London Philharmonic Orchestra before the Queen at the Royal Festival Hall. The *Guardian* described the Master of the Queen's Music as a prolific composer of finished and unfinished works and the LPO and Mr Haitink, the conductor, felt that it would be improper to perform an incomplete work.

However the *Mass* was duly completed and John was involved in further delicate negotiations when it was proposed that the full work should be performed by the Festival Chorus and the Royal Philharmonic Orchestra in Westminster Cathedral on 17th February 1978. This was a formidable undertaking because the Festival Chorus is not a permanent body as each host director auditions and forms the chorus each year. Cathedral lay clerks are the only singers guaranteed a place and the 'home' team tend to provide more singers than the other two cathedrals. To gather the Chorus together for rehearsals and a performance out of season would be no easy matter.

A full discussion was held in Ledbury on 5th October 1977 by the three cathedral organists and John Bimson – the concert organiser for the RPO – about the proposed performance, when it was agreed that they should go ahead and contact the Chorus in order to ascertain their response. However before this was done Donald Hunt wrote to John about his anxieties. He pointed out that Worcester had already agreed with Argo to make two records during the period 15th–18th February and it would therefore be impossible for the Worcester lay clerks to take part in a London concert. He also suggested that the rehearsal time listed in John's proposals would be insufficient to produce a worthy Three Choirs performance. He pointed out that even in the Gloucester performance there were moments which were far from correct and 'there was much tentative singing'. He added that an extra 'London' pressure and a 'six month forgetting period' all pointed to a wholly inadequate preparation time. Members of his chorus had already expressed their uneasiness about the success of such a performance. What further concerned Donald was the question of who was going to pay for it all: 'Certainly the RPO will not!' His final comment was about his anxiety that 'this miserable piece' might continue to insult the good name and standards of the Festival and the people associated with it: 'Poor showing in London could do untold damage, not least to my efforts next August.'

By 2nd November, Roy Massey of Hereford was also beginning to have qualms. He had already mentioned his concerns about the extra work involved, in view of a major March concert in Hereford and was also reluctant to release the lay clerks from a full Friday choir practice only a week after half-term. He also was preparing for an Abbey recording and a BBC programme around that time. 'Speaking personally,' he wrote,

> I am not terribly enthusiastic about the idea, as I feel the summer build-up of the enthusiastic hard work and the tremendous atmosphere of the week itself generates an impetus which takes the chorus more or less safely through the musical hazards. I do wonder whether we can pull it off in quite the same way in the dark days of mid-February, in the quite appalling acoustic of Westminster Cathedral, which is a depressing barn of a place at the best of times. Were you conducting the event, I should feel compelled to support you with all my might, as we are all in this together, but I cannot feel quite so enthusiastic for someone else.

Roy Massey ended his letter with a characteristic appeal to the whole nature of the Three Choirs:

> The Festival completely dominates my summer, both in my work with the Cathedral choir and, of course, with our chorus contingent, and I flog very hard indeed to try and knock the notes into my country town choralists. I am quite happy to do this, as I feel privileged indeed to be part of such a wonderful institution, but it is something of a relief to settle down in the autumn to two terms of domestic music-making, and I am therefore none too keen that the Festival – wonderful though it is – should intrude itself into our Spring-time activities.

In the event the Festival chorus did perform the completed *Mass of Christ the King* on 3rd November 1978 in Westminster Cathedral under the baton of Sir Charles Groves with the Royal Philharmonic Orchestra. It was one of the very few times in two hundred and fifty years that the Three Choirs Festival Chorus has sung outside the Festival itself and certainly outside the three counties of Gloucester, Hereford and Worcester.

Also in 1978 John received a handwritten letter from Malcolm Williamson about the Gloucester Three Choirs in 1977: 'You behaved with the patience of a saint and with a professionalism that I appreciate deeply. I see by hindsight the quandary in which I placed you – obliging you to present a work which you had prepared chorally wherein four of the sixteen movements were not orchestrated . . . your kindness to me when I was tiresome was amazing!' So often has that been the experience of those who have dealings with John.

An appreciative letter to John was also received from the Orchestra da Camera after the Festival: 'It was great to read so appreciative an account in the Musical Times about your fine direction of the whole Festival. All I can say is that from start to finish you were more than equal to the whole occasion. Certainly nobody could possibly have guessed at the B Minor Mass on the Wednesday how many other things you had on your mind. And we loved working for you in it.'

In many ways the 1977 anniversary Festival established John's reputation, not only as an outstanding Musical Director who could maintain the morale of a professional orchestra as well as the soloists and essentially amateur chorus but also as one who remained calm and courteous under the most demanding of situations. Soon after this, he became seriously ill with a life-threatening illness which he faced up to with equal resolution, faith and equanimity

The Three Choirs Triumvirate – John Sanders, Roy Massey and
Donald Hunt – presented to Queen Elizabeth, the Queen Mother
in Westminster Cathedral, 1978

although at times he was in severe pain and with threatened
disability. The radium treatment was successful but it meant
missing the Hereford Festival as well as leaving the Gloucester choir to the amiable expertise of Andrew Millington, at
the time assistant organist. He had a relapse with the
Hodgkin's disease in 1981 which caused further anxiety, but
only Janet knew how serious it all was.

Gloucester 1980

In spite of being seriously ill which many would have felt
justified taking things easily, plans for the next Festival at
Gloucester were being made almost as soon as that most
demanding 1977 Festival had been successfully completed.
One of the features of John's time in Gloucester was the
increasing number of performances taking place in venues

around the city and county and this in itself demanded meticulous and careful planning. Not only did Tewkesbury Abbey become a regular host for Three Choirs perform-ances, but the Roman Catholic Benedictine monastery at Prinknash Abbey was taking a full part along with other exhi-bitions, lectures, displays and chamber music recitals. All these were included in the 1980 Festival amongst the more conventional favourites and newly commissioned works.

For the first time the Gloucestershire Youth Orchestra, under Mark Foster, performed on the eve of the opening service, and so successful and popular were they that it became a regular assignment. The City of Birmingham Symphony Orchestra took part in a majestic performance of *The Kingdom*, conducted by John Sanders, and The City of London Sinfonia was conducted by Richard Hickox. Echoing earlier times there was a request in the programme notes for *The Kingdom* that there should be no applause until after the work had ended, perhaps indicating that a new less cognisant audience was now being attracted to the Festival. Sharing the main performances of the week with the CBSO was the Royal Philharmonic Orchestra who accompanied the first performance of *Lord of Light* by Philip Cannon, conducted by John. There is an interesting local touch in this work for the final movement, *Christe Redemptor Omnium*, is sung by soloists and chorus to the plainsong of the chimes of Gloucester Cathedral on Fridays at 8 a.m., 1 p.m. and 5 p.m. They were originally chimed soon after the building of the tower in 1450 and restored to use in 1979. One of the soloists for this concert was Penelope Walker, a former pupil of John's at the Ladies' College, Cheltenham. Also in the same programme was a recently discovered Haydn *St Nicholas Mass* conducted by Roy Massey, followed by Wagner's *Wesendonck Lieder* and Walton's *Symphony No. 1*.

The Three Choirs finished on the Saturday evening with Bizet's *Te Deum* and the Sibelius *Karelia Suite* conducted by Roy Massey and Janacek's *Glagolitic Mass* conducted by John Sanders as the finale. Other orchestras and consortia taking part during the week were the Orchestra of St John's, Smith Square, the New London Consort and the Orchestra da Camera. A new sound was heard at the Gloucestershire College of Education with a Fresh Ear concert given by electronic instruments in which the programme included *Tongs and Bones* and the world premiere of Wiegold's *New Work*.

Gloucester 1983

The special occasion commemorated at this Festival was the granting of a Charter of Incorporation to Gloucester five hundred years previously by King Richard III. Gloucester was not yet a city and that had to wait until the abbey became a cathedral in 1541, but the town burgesses now had the right to elect a mayor and 12 aldermen. Richard had been Duke of Gloucester before he seized the throne and it was natural that he should seek to show favour on the town and his act allowed it to have a significant amount of independence in creating its prosperity.

The city of Gloucester celebrated the Charter by commissioning a special work by the Gloucester-born Richard Shepherd, ex-chorister of the cathedral and later headmaster of the York Minster Choir School. Richard has been a prolific composer of church and secular music, whose *Preces and Responses* are sung in cathedrals around the world and who was to compose a large work for the four hundred and fiftieth anniversary of the re-foundation of the King's School by King Henry VIII. The commemoration work *Let Us Now Praise Famous Men* (from Ecclesiasticus, chapter 44) was performed by the St Cecilia Singers, a highly expert group based at the cathedral, of whom Janet Sanders was a long-standing member, and conducted by Andrew Millington, who had been responsible for the choir when he was assistant organist. Appropriately the whole concert was in praise of Gloucestershire men with Finzi's *Magnificat* and Christopher Steele's *Six Pieces for Organ* included, along with some of Elgar's part-songs to recall a much-loved Festival supporter. Elsewhere during the week Ivor Gurney was remembered in a lecture by Michael Hurd on *The Man and his Music*.

Another innovative and notable concert came the next evening when John Sanders conducted Howard Ferguson's *Amore Langueo*, the words of which were composed in the fourteenth century. Ferguson dedicated his work to Gerald and Joyce Finzi and it was Finzi's *Concerto for Clarinet and Strings* which followed, conducted by Donald Hunt who also conducted Elgar's *The Music Makers*. This concert was recorded by the BBC for transmission on Radio Three which, alas, has become a more rare event in recent times.

Again the Royal Philharmonic Orchestra shared the main concerts with the City of Birmingham Symphony Orchestra and once again, Sir Charles Groves conducted an orchestral concert which included Wagner's *Parsifal*, *Job* by Vaughan Williams and a rare *Concerto for Organ, Strings and Percussion* by Charles Camilleri. The other main visiting conductor was Simon Rattle who conducted the CBSO in Benjamin Britten's *Sinfonia da Requiem* and Mahler's *Symphony No. 10*.

John Sanders however, as Director of the Festival, took the lion's share of the conducting and, apart from the BBC recording, conducted the opening service and two of the Choral Evensongs and then on the Monday evening,

Wagner's *Siegfried Idyll* and the much-acclaimed *Mass of the Sea* by Paul Patterson which was commissioned by the Three Choirs Festival with help from the Arts Council. On Tuesday evening he led the Royal Philharmonic Orchestra in Bax's *Tintagel*, followed by Elgar's *Sea Pictures Op. 37* and on the Wednesday was again with the RPO and the Festival Chorus conducting Strauss's *Four Last Songs* and Brahms' *Ein Deutsches Requiem.* Finally on the last evening he was at it again with quite different music, the joyful and exuberant *Carmina Burana* by Carl Orff. This work had at first been forbidden in the cathedral by the Dean and Chapter, recalling the nineteenth-century days when Deans and Chapters looked askance at any slightly wayward or disrespectful frivolity by Three Choirs administration.

It is easy to take the work of the Festival Director for granted and John always appeared to be so relaxed and calm and take things as a matter of course that one could overlook the immense amount of work and anxiety which must have been present at a time when much had to be beyond his control. An astonishing aspect of the Three Choirs was that there was a party at 7 Miller's Green every evening before and after a concert on the occasions when the committee and sponsors were not giving one. The stamina and easy friendliness of John and Janet was quite outstanding on these occasions when the hospitality went beyond the path of duty.

Gloucester 1986

As a result of the experience and close relationship of the three cathedral organists, there was by this time a growing confidence to introduce new music and fringe events into an ever-growing Festival. However, in spite of the main events being continually sold out, patrons were now being warned of the costs involved in maintaining the Festival and enabling it to compete with other major festivals which were rapidly growing around the country. Christian Wilson, honorary secretary of the Gloucester team, wrote that 'less than half the cost of mounting the events at this festival is met by the price of the tickets' and that the Festival officers, all of whom are voluntary workers, 'wear out their knees begging from commercial sponsors without whose generous support we could not hope to run a major festival of quality'.

It was therefore some comfort that, thanks to John Sanders' programme, the BBC undertook to record two concerts, one with the Festival Chorus and the Royal Philharmonic Orchestra when Roy Massey conducted Walton's *Coronation Te Deum* and the *Introduction and Allegro for Strings* by Elgar and John Sanders conducted Berlioz's *Les*

The Three Choirs Festival Choir

Nuits d'été and a performance of Paul Patterson's *Stabat Mater*. The latter had been commissioned by the Huddersfield Choral Society as part of their 150th anniversary celebrations and had been performed by them earlier. Unhappily in one of the movements the chorus had sung a whole section a minor third below the note and the BBC hoped that the Three Choirs would make a better job of it. They did get it right and Anthony Boden observed that 'John Sanders secured a fine performance.' Kenneth Loveland wrote of the music that, 'Paul Patterson writes music that strikes home ... the sort of new music that the choral tradition needs if it is to survive.'

Another new work which provoked rather more controversy was Andrew Lloyd Webber's *Requiem* which had already enjoyed two hundred and fifty seven performances around the world, sold over half a million records and in which the soprano/tenor duet *Hosanna* reached third place in the pop charts. The John Sanders performance in the cathedral was deemed to be 'convincing' and Kenneth Loveland wrote in its defence that 'the elements of jazz and pop are not out of place. Mr Lloyd Webber is writing in the idiom in which he best expresses himself, and it is never superficial music.' One young chorister, Douglas Mason, now teaching music at the specialist music school Chethams in Manchester, became 'the darling of the matrons in the Pie Jesu duet', according to Douglas Drane in the Gloucester *Citizen* newspaper. On the whole the efforts of the conductor, the Royal Liverpool Philharmonic Orchestra and Festival Chorus were applauded for their efforts in spite of the protest of traditionalists that it was not a suitable piece for the Festival. Anthony Boden quotes a review by Barrie Grayson who wrote a damning criticism of the work while applauding the efforts of the performers: 'John Sanders, Miriam Bowen,

Arthur Davies, Master Douglas Mason, Chorus and Orchestra (the RLPO) gave their all to a work which owes more to the popularity of the composer than in this instance, the quality of the music. This easily forgotten work with its borrowings and gimmicky pastiche sounds as if it were conceived bar by bar at the piano and passed on to a synthesizer expert for up-market sound colour.'

For regular Three Choirs supporters the complete performance of Malcolm Williamson's *Mass of Christ the King* came as a welcome climax, not least to the composer. 'It is terribly moving to have the work performed here in Gloucester after what happened in 1977,' he told Douglas Drane. 'I would like to thank John Sanders, Donald Hunt and Roy Massey for keeping faith with me. Not everyone was so understanding. I was lambasted by the Press for not getting it finished in time in 1977 and, in my opinion, I think I was unfairly treated. Still, I suppose when you are Master of the Queen's music, you have to expect something like that. The Royal Family have to put up with it, so why should I complain?'

Another first came on the Wednesday afternoon when the well-established Jane Glover became the first female conductor of a major work at the Gloucester Festival when she guided the London Mozart Players through Haydn and Mozart Symphonies and a *Concerto for Oboe d'Amore and Strings* by a rising twentieth-century composer, Mary Chandler, who not only read English at Oxford but was principal oboist in the City of Birmingham Symphony Orchestra. This was followed by the 'severe test' of Mahler's Eighth Symphony in the evening, conducted by John Sanders. Writing in the *Guardian*, Barry Still commented:

> If it is axiomatic these days that cathedral organists, as well as their routine round of services, can cope adequately with

conducting major quasi-liturgical works and oratorios such as Beethoven's *Missa Solemnis* and Mendelssohn's *Elijah* (both of which were performed at this Three Choirs Festival under John Sanders), there is no guarantee that they will be just as successful with a piece like Mahler's Eighth Symphony. Yet marshalling the huge forces with composure and poise, he achieved triumphantly a reading of immense power and persuasion.

He went on to describe the effect.

This came about through effective synthesis of the pacing of the sections, shading dynamics, revelation of the orchestral hues and conception of the unity as both symphonic and imaginative statement. In Part One the rhythmic thrust was delivered with assurance, the problem of growth within the immense fugue solved with cogency. And despite clouded textures and earlier climaxes, the sonic waves of the Gloria flowed with sense of spiritual and mental exaltation. Sanders disclosed the seemingly limitless melodic edifice with spontaneity, eagerly supported by chorus, cathedral trebles and soloists. The Royal Philharmonic Orchestra, finishing its Festival duty, passed the severe test with credit, strings velvety, brass noble without stridency.[7]

In many ways the intensely full and demanding 1986 Festival and Mahler's Eighth in particular marked the zenith of John Sanders' career as a master musician in full control of his craft, recognised by professionals, amateurs and music lovers alike. Mark Blatchly summed up this moment from his advantageous position in the organ loft: 'I shall always cherish my favourite memory of John, the Royal Philharmonic rising as one to its feet with the chorus, soloists and audience to give him an ovation for the magisterial reading of Mahler's mighty Eighth Symphony. I still see him beaming with delight and typically, for he is modest to a fault, with genuine surprise that the glory of the accomplished triumph should be reflected upon him.'

I met John behind the stage just after the performance, which he admitted was 'special'. I asked him how he was feeling after such an enthusiastic reception. His answer was characteristically simple from an exhausted man, 'Alan, I just can't wait for that final D major chord (from *Elijah*) on Saturday evening.'

Nevertheless John went on to conduct the Gloucester contingent of the Festival Chorus with the London Mozart Players in the quite different *Petite Messe Solonelle* by Rossini the next afternoon. The *Citizen* music critic Douglas Drane described the work as a 'much needed little light relief' after the huge exertions of Williamson and Mahler and reported that 'there were smiles all round' with 'feet tapping in time with the music'. Nevertheless there was no relaxation for John as the Chorus were well aware that he had to work extra hard to make the London Mozart Players put the required amount of jollity and zip into the work. That he did so successfully was summed up by the newspaper review: 'Had the concert been in the theatre we would have insisted on encores from soloists and chorus.'

Despite increasing tiredness, the final concert, *Elijah*, with another chorister treble, Andrew Wooldridge, joining with Helen Walker (soprano), John's former pupil Penelope Walker (mezzo-soprano), Maldwyn Davies (tenor) and the popular Three Choirs Festival bass, Brian Raynor Cook, was another triumph recognised as such by a musically insatiated audience. At the end of it all, as orchestra, Festival officials and Chorus went round to Miller's Green for the inevitable lavish and final party in the organist's house, we saw the ever-watchful and practical Janet driving a weary John away into the night, having decided it was best to leave everyone else to rejoice in his reflected glory.

Gloucester 1989

By 1989, after some twenty-two years as Director, John Sanders' original views about the Festival had become clearly defined: 'We wouldn't wish to present ourselves as another Edinburgh. This is probably – apart maybe from Norwich – the only festival still to base itself on the large choral work. This choral tradition lies at the heart of amateur music making and is something that doesn't need importing. All the voices come from here on our own doorstep.'

With his ever-increasing love for Gloucestershire, John, as the Festival Director, ensured that one of its most eminent musical sons should have pride of place. Sir Hubert Parry's *Prometheus Unbound* was first performed in Gloucester on 7th December 1880, and it is claimed by Jeremy Dibble who wrote an appreciation of Parry in the 1989 programme, that the piece marked a new beginning in English music. Sir Herbert Howells said that 'the year of the *Prometheus Unbound* is accounted the time of our escape from Mendelssohnian captivity, the year of renaissance in English music'. Although this work was not included, no fewer than six of Parry's other works were performed, with a lecture by Michael Kennedy on the composer. Interestingly enough, John Sanders only conducted the canticles during the opening service and left other works to his associate conductors Roy Massey and Donald Hunt. The Gloucestershire Youth Orchestra under Mark Foster, a now established part of the Three Choirs Festival, played Parry's *Symphony No. 5* and the English String Orchestra under Mark Boughton performed the rarely heard *Lady Radnor's Suite*. As well as encouraging and commissioning new music, the Three Choirs Festival has ensured that a good deal of worthy music has been kept alive. This was carefully maintained during the time of the triumvirate of John Sanders, Roy Massey and Donald Hunt.

As well as restoring Parry to his proper place in the English repertoire this Festival was also adventurous with other little-heard music. Zoltan Kodaly's *Budavari Te Deum*, Elis Pehkonen's *Russian Requiem* and John Rutter's *Requiem* based on the 1662 Book of Common Prayer rather than the Roman Mass were performed during the week, the latter being conducted by the composer with the Royal Liverpool Philharmonic Orchestra. Alas an organ concerto by Michael Berkeley, due to be played by Gillian Weir, had to be postponed to another Festival on account of three missing notes on Gloucester's organ keyboard. Gillian had tried to persuade the composer to revise his work but it proved to be too difficult in the time left before the concert.

Three massive works conducted by John Sanders were performed during the week and each received a tremendous acclaim. The first was Elgar's *The Kingdom* when the Festival Chorus was 'almost faultless' with the RPO and 'brought a deep sense of spirituality to the work'. Indeed there was 'near to a revival meeting atmosphere as the emotions were so stirred'. A professional musician friend from London remarked that he had never, ever heard such a powerful performance. There was an atmosphere of expectancy throughout the week, especially noticeable when John conducted the Verdi *Requiem* and this reached a dramatic climax on the final evening when the Chorus and the RLPO united in a spirited performance of Elgar's nationalistic oratorio *Caractacus*. The capacity audience joined in a full-blooded rendering of Parry's *Jerusalem* as a finale to the week's Festival.

Gloucester 1992

With hindsight it seemed most fitting that John Sanders' last two Festivals as Director should coincide with anniversaries of two of the county's most famous composers. Hubert Parry's anniversary was followed in 1992 with that of Herbert Howells who not only loved the three 'magic' cathedrals of the Three Choirs but also became a major composer of church music during his later years. It seems odd therefore that while the opening service used the Sanders *Responses*, Walmsley's *Magnificat and Nunc Dimittis for Double Choir in B Flat Major* was preferred to one of the Howells great settings for the canticles. However this was made up for during the week with Howells' deeply moving, strongly Anglican *Requiem*, which contains the favourite 23rd and 121st psalms as well as the graveside, funeral response from the Book of Revelation, 'I heard a voice from heaven, saying unto me, Write from henceforth blessed are the dead which die in the Lord. Even so saith the Spirit, for they rest from their labours.'

A fitting arrangement of local masters came on the Friday afternoon when Herbert Howells' *Organ Sonata*, played by Francis Grier, was performed before an evening concert when John Sanders was conducting Sir Herbert Brewer's *Emmaus* with the Festival Chorus and the Royal Liverpool Philharmonic Orchestra. A secular work by Howells, *A Kent Yeoman's Wooing Song*, appeared earlier in the week conducted by Donald Hunt, who also conducted his *Sine Nomine*, a work first performed in Gloucester Cathedral in 1922 when the composer himself conducted the London Symphony Orchestra. Also performed was Howells' *Rhapsodic Quintet* and his *Violin Concerto.*

On the Tuesday evening during Evensong a window in memory of Herbert Howells designed by Caroline Swash was dedicated. The window displays settings for the canticles as well as references to other works such as *Hymnus Paradisi* and his anthem *Like as the Hart*. However the anthem sung at the service was a new one by John Rutter, *Hymn to the Creator of Light*.

Loyal as ever to the county and to the Three Choirs twentieth-century tradition, there were plenty of works by local composers, Finzi in particular and Philip Cannon, and John's own *In Praise of Gloucestershire*, dedicated 'with great affection to my wife Janet and our two children Anna and Jonathan, who, together with the countryside, provided the inspiration for this music'.

Of course there were well-known works by famous composers, amongst them Brahms (*Academic Festival Overture*), Sibelius (*Three Pieces for the Fire Brigade Band*), Rachmaninov (*Vespers – All Night Vigil*), Debussey (*La Cathedrale Engloutle and L'Isle Joyeuse*), Mendelssohn (*Sechs Spruche zum Kirchenjahr, Psalm 22*) and Duruflé (*Requiem*).

The works at the main evening concerts conducted by John were as varied as ever. First there was Patterson's *Mass of the Sea*, threatening to become a hardy annual, Bach's mighty *Mass in B Minor* with the Brandenberg Consort and Festival Chorus and as a grand finale to the Festival and to John's directorship of it what else but Elgar's *Dream of Gerontius*, a regular must at the Three Choirs Festival.

During this Festival John knew that it was going to be his last. His conducting shoulder was becoming very painful and he was aware that if he wanted to make time for composing, he would have to give up the pressures and unremitting routine of the round of services, the enormous planning and preparation for the world's oldest music festival and his teaching at the Ladies' College.

Coming to Gloucester when he did, the prospect of taking over at a time when the great names of English music – Parry, Elgar, Vaughan Williams and Howells – were vanishing from the Three Choirs scene, must have been daunting. There were constant press observations that the Festival had had its day, the increasing cost of obtaining the best orchestras and performers was becoming very demanding and also the requirements of training a chorus who had the experience, expertise and stamina to sing a punishing schedule of difficult music at the highest standards were there to challenge the abilities of the finest musicians and directors. The fact that the Festival has remained as popular as ever with an increasingly popular appeal is a tribute to John and his fellow directors, Roy Massey of Hereford and Donald Hunt of Worcester. Although they were supported by good local committees who accepted very demanding roles, it remains true that the three cathedral organists were the only full-time organisers and the Three Choirs Festival ultimately depended on them. Towards the end of his life, John became even more convinced that the future well-being of the Festival depended on the three local directors and when he learned that the American conductor, Leonard Slatkin, was due to conduct Elgar's *Kingdom* at the 1999 Festival he responded with rare ferocity: 'What does Leonard Slatkin know about this music? In the old days the cathedral organists used to do all the conducting. There was a tradition in the way things were done'.

A glance at any Festival programme indicates just how much music is presented during the week. Is there any other gathering in the world which brings together so many of the highest artists and orchestras and offers so much classical choral music of international quality and yet retains a strong local and even parochial atmosphere?

Chapter Seven
The Compositions

Herbert Howells, a former articled pupil of Dr Sir Herbert Brewer in Gloucester Cathedral, once urged all musicians to give of their best to the Church for the glory of God. This advice John Sanders took to heart, especially in his latter days when, in formal retirement, he devoted himself to producing a large amount of church music. He was also commissioned to write secular music, especially in connection with his beloved, adopted county, Gloucestershire, whose composers and poets he did so much to promote.

It is quite certain that John would have arranged and composed short pieces for the choir and choral society of Gonville and Caius as well as the Cambridge University Second Orchestra which he conducted, but such works have been lost apart from a set of *Responses for Evensong* which were arranged by John, based on the famous and most popular Smith of Durham responses.

Thus his first known composition, *My Beloved Spake*, was written in 1958, the year he came to Gloucester for the first time. As with most of his compositions, it was written for a particular occasion in response to requests from friends or choral societies. In this case it was written for the marriage of a college friend, Andrew Taylor, and Pauline. The first performance was at their wedding in Nottingham on 5th September 1958. The choir was made up of the choral exhibitioners of Gonville and Caius, with the trebles from the local parish church. It is a reminder of those far-off days when parish church choirs were often capable of singing sophisticated and difficult music. And *My Beloved Spake* was no exception. It begins with treble voices introducing the speaker and continues with the four parts expressing the meaning of the words and the developing springtime of a relationship in a way that was to become a hallmark of John's writing. Already he had begun to use dissonant chords to emphasise important words as in the 'Arise, rise up' and the final 'Come away', sung by the men's voices, as if the groom is taking charge of his bride after she has been given away by her father. Some beautiful passages when 'winter is past' and 'the flowers are appearing on earth' are in the Lydian mode of soft luxurious and gentle passion, much beloved by John in his later work.

Undoubtedly his choice of words was inspired by the fine anthem, using the same words from the Song of Songs, written by his composition teacher, Patrick Hadley, Professor of Music at Cambridge:

> *My beloved spake, and said unto me,*
> *Rise up, my love, my fair one, and come away,*
> *For, lo, the winter is past,*
> *The rain is over and gone;*
> *The flowers appear on the earth;*
> *The time of the singing of birds is come,*
> *And the voice of the turtle is heard in our land;*
> *The fig tree putteth forth her green figs,*
> *And the vines are in blossom,*
> *They give forth their fragrance.*
> *Arise, my love, my fair one, and come away.*

The piece was finally published in 2001 by Banks Publications.[1]

Although most of John Sanders' most serious works were produced when he had more leisure to put his mind to them, there were nonetheless some very significant early compositions which indicated a definite quality and style. One such was the *Festival Te Deum*, written at the request of the Cheltenham Bach Society in 1960, which has become part of the standard repertoire of cathedral choirs around the world. On entering Christchurch Cathedral in New Zealand in 2007, I heard the choir practising it for the great Festival of Flowers which is held in February each year.

The rousing opening fanfare introduces an exciting choral introduction of rising chords, expressing joyous praise and worship rising to a magnificent climax with the 'Holy, Holy, Holy'. New themes are developed to fit the changing moods of the work with wonderful dissonant harmonies to emphasise the important words and then a quieter, reflective theme is used to bring out the awesome meaning of the phrase 'We believe that thou shalt come to be our judge'. The first theme comes back with the sopranos and altos introducing the joyous 'Day by day we magnify thee' and leading up to the final 'O Lord in thee have I trusted: let me never be confounded'.

The *Te Deum* was first performed in Cheltenham College Chapel, conducted by the composer with Herbert Sumsion at the organ. Later, at Sumsion's request, John orchestrated the work so that it could be sung by the Festival Chorus accompanied by the London Symphony Orchestra at the opening service of the Gloucester Three Choirs Festival in 1962. The following morning Frank Howes commented in *The Times*, 'John Sanders conducted his *Te Deum*, a splendid setting composed for the occasion [sic]. It owes – at any rate for the purposes of description and categorisation – something to Walton; it is sustained on a pervasive swaying figure suggestive of bells and it is modern in its well-judged use of clanging dissonance; its scoring is clear and well adapted to a large church.'

Anna Turmeau, in her intriguing dissertation on John Sanders' music, echoes his judgement but adds, 'In this both attractive and effective early liturgical setting Sanders sounds a convincing individual compositional voice. Although steeped in the Anglican liturgical tradition of Wood and Stanford it exudes the vitality and harmonic freshness of Walton's *Coronation Te Deum* and the melodic lyricism of Britten's earlier *Festival Te Deum* setting.'[2]

The composer suggested that Britten may have had an influence on the 'extrovert style' of the work and 'although I did not know it at the time, I seem to have quoted an arpeggio figure from Walton's *Te Deum*'. He went on to say that it was written for a big chorus and, 'although we do it with the cathedral choir, I sometimes feel a bit sorry for the altos and boys having to go up to top A-flats and B-flats'.

Although there were so many worthy settings of the *Te Deum* around, this one became a popular worldwide work and after its publication by the Oxford University Press in 1962, it sold over 2200 copies in the first five years, of which half were purchased by overseas choirs.

Another liturgical best-seller was produced much later but enjoyed even wider circulation around the world. This was John's *Preces and Responses* published by the RSCM Press in 1989 and dedicated to 'the choirs affiliated to the Royal School of Church Music in the Gloucester Diocese'. These *Responses* also commemorate the centenary of the death of Richard Wagner in 1883. They are based on the

Dresden Amen, used extensively by Wagner in his Music Drama *Parsifal*. These *Responses* have become part of the regular repertoire of many choirs around the world and up to the end of 2003 some 15,000 copies were sold in Canada, the United States, Australia and New Zealand as well as Great Britain.

At least one young chorister, a certain Hamish Charters, counted these *Responses* amongst his favourites and told John, when he was in Worcester to present the chorister awards, that he liked them 'because they made good sense and some of the notes took you by surprise'. Certainly they have a contemporary sound, are sufficiently difficult to be demanding and yet are accessible.

Mention has been made of John's overseas sales and, after successful tours by Gloucester Cathedral Choir down the eastern seaboard of the United States, John was able to have some of his works published in America. He was offered

John with Janet and Joan Wake Cleveland at the investiture of his doctorate, 1990

help by Sir David Willcocks who, at the time, was an editor of English Cathedral Music for the American market and who gave him advice not only about the nature of American choirs but also about how to invest the royalties he might receive. For a person as careful and meticulous as John the financial advice was very well received.

Amongst the music were three prayers which he sent to Lorenz, publishers in Dayton, Ohio.[3] The first was *The Prayer of St Francis*, originally composed in 1989 for the choir of Gloucestershire Royal Hospital, probably at the instigation of Dr Jim Hoyland who was very active in the Three Choirs Festival with John for many years. The words, which may not come directly from St Francis himself but have been attributed to him for some centuries, are:

Merciful God, to thee we commend ourselves and all those
   who need thy help and correction.
Where there is hatred, give love;
Where there is injury, pardon ;
Where there is doubt, faith;
Where there is despair, hope;
Where there is sadness, joy;
Where there is darkness, light.
Grant that we may not seek so much to be consoled, as to
   console;
To be understood, as to understand;
To be loved, as to love;
For in giving, we receive, in pardoning we are pardoned,
   and dying we are born into eternal life.

The other work was *The Prayer of St Richard*, a long favourite with English congregations and school assemblies:

> *Thanks be to Thee, my Lord Jesus Christ,*
> *For all the benefits which thou hast given me,*
> *For all the pains and insults which thou hast borne for me.*
> *O most merciful Redeemer, Friend and Brother,*
> *May I know you more clearly,*
> *Love you more dearly,*
> *And follow you more nearly*
> *Now and for evermore.*

The writing of music for these two prayers and much of his other music tells us something about John's spirituality and inner life. Most of us brought up in an English culture are rather cautious and reticent about openly expressing our religious convictions as we regard them as part of our personal private life. But there is no doubt that John found tremendous value in the use of traditional prayers like the ones above as well as the time-honoured liturgy of the Anglican Church. One of the saving graces, in his view, of the liturgical amendments and 'modern' forms of worship in the second half of the twentieth century was that the service of Evensong was left alone and even the most avant-garde canons of cathedrals were content with the 1662 service. Attempts at revising it in modern form have demonstrated that it cannot be bettered and even the revision of the lessons and psalms has been modified by many. In the case of the psalms there is a danger that contemporary choirs will lose the skill of singing them with real effect and understanding as they can get away with a dozen verses each evening. The latest liturgical calendar offers the same psalms four times in the fortnight at certain seasons of the year.

While some cathedral organists and writers of church

music have remained agnostics throughout their careers –
Herbert Sumsion and Ralph Vaughan Williams immediately
spring to mind in the Gloucester context – John was most
certainly a confirmed believer who prayed through his
music which was itself a reflection of the ancient liturgy.

The third prayer, *Day by Day*, was turned down by the
American publishers as 'not being saleable'. Correspondence between Sir David Willcocks and John suggests that
this may have been because it was 'in a more difficult class'.
Apparently the American choirs do not respond eagerly to
music involving top As and B flat in the soprano/treble line.
In fact Sir David had warned John that this might be the case
but John, although tempted, stuck to his revised score: 'I
originally wrote it in G but transposed it into A flat as I
thought it would sound better. Perhaps it would have been
better to leave it as it was.'

Another piece of liturgical music published in the United
States was his *Deus Misereatur – God be Merciful Unto Us
and Bless Us* which had originally been commissioned by
John Brooks, an American who became a lay clerk in
Gloucester Cathedral for a year. It was to mark the retirement of Dr Anthony Crossland, Organist of Wells Cathedral
in July 1996.

In composing this work John mentioned that there were
not many good settings of this favourite *Psalm 67* which had
dropped out of use as a result of the displacement of Sung
Matins in favour of the Eucharist for the morning service but
was still a popular choice at weddings. The editor of the
Sacred Music Press in New York who had received the music
from Geoff Lorenz, President of Lorenz Publishing Company,
described it as 'a joy'.

Another psalm published in the United States which was
received with considerable enthusiasm was a setting of the

Jubilate Deo. This was also sent off to the Seoul Music Company for publication in Korea. Once again Sir David Willcocks warned that the American publisher might baulk at a top A in the service and pointed out that this might be overcome by giving the sopranos an F sharp, taking the alto to A and the tenor to D with the bass to complete the chord. John replied that he had 'included a little divisi work as we agreed, mostly in the soprano parts' and had aimed to 'keep the style as simple as possible but at the same time to provide some harmonic and rhythmic interest'. This was obviously acceptable and it was published as part of an English Cathedral Music series for Lorenz. It is interesting that the company asked for music which would be within the reach of the 'average organist' and would not require too much time in preparation, a reminder of the uniqueness of the English cathedral tradition with its professional choirs who can usually manage highly sophisticated and intricate music without too much difficulty. The Americans have very few professional choirs.

Other works first published in the United States were *The Promised Messiah*, *My Dancing Day*, *Blessed be the Maid Mary* and in due course the prayer originally rejected, *Day by Day*.

Partly as a result of a presentation of English Church Music at the American Guild of Organists' Convention and the tours by the Gloucester Cathedral Choir of the USA under the direction of John, his music sold very well. Just how highly he and his music were regarded is reflected in the sales. Between the publication of his first pieces in 1989 and 2002 over 15,000 copies of the *Jubilate Deo* were sold in America with a number going to other countries overseas. *The Prayer of St Francis* sold over 10,000, *The Promised Messiah* sales reached over 5000 copies and even the originally rejected piece *Day by Day* sold more than 3000 within four years of its publication. Given the fairly narrow and limited appeal of liturgical music today these are notable statistics, especially at a time when there have been a large number of new compositions, following the constant revision and modernising of church services since 1965. One measure of the success of the enterprise of having music published and sold in the United States was that John soon found it worthwhile to open a bank account in the USA to avoid the caprices and uncertainties of the financial exchange rates. No doubt this was useful on his excursions with the choir.

During the last decade of the twentieth century several publishers were anxious to commission music from John, one of the principal ones being Encore Publications. Tim Rogers, the publisher and composer of religious and secular music, wrote of how 'his music always makes a profound impact on an audience. And I have a lasting memory of hearing his *Requiem* in Keble College Chapel in March 2001 when we were both represented as composers in a programme given by the choir Commotio.'

One of the major pieces published by Encore was the anthem *Come My Way* which was written for the enthronement of Rowan Williams as Archbishop of Wales and used later in his enthronement as Archbishop of Canterbury and thus heard throughout the English-speaking world.

There is a story about this work. We have already seen that John was very much at home in putting traditional prayers and liturgy to music and this is no exception. My wife, Frances, asked John if he would write a short anthem for a little village choir I had started (possibly rather foolishly!) in a tiny, remote village church in Radnorshire. Shortage of young people meant that we depended on farmers and farmers' wives who had little experience of singing anything. Nevertheless we had a go with often quite difficult music by Tallis and Orlando Gibbons and others from the Church Anthem Book edited by Walford Davies and Henry Ley, published by Oxford. John was aware of this and came up with an anthem, *The Call*, words by George Herbert, consisting of three parts: sopranos, altos and men's voices. The first verse is for sopranos only to bring out the melody. Subsequent verses become more demanding with a change of key and the familiar dissonant chords giving emphasis, with a glorious fortissimo climax in E♭ major with a chromatic line from the altos. It was published in *Fourteen New Anthems for SA and Men* by Kevin Mayhew in 1997 as part of the publisher's urgent desire to make the Church and its music more accessible to the general populace.

In our minuscule Welsh village we were thrilled to learn that *The Call* was to be sung at our Archbishop's enthronement but of course by then John had developed it into a quite different and difficult work for a 'proper' choir with a full orchestration.

Perhaps at this stage, when we have reached a work that John composed for a humble little parish choir as well as for one of the most majestic of church services, an assessment of how and why John composed is now appropriate.

In the second half of the twentieth century there was a new and serious questioning about what the Church stood for in an age which was clearly becoming more secular. When John arrived in Gloucester for the first time, the Anglican liturgy was unchanged from the seventeenth century and even a modern, scholarly translation of the Bible had not yet been published. In many churches and cathedrals Matins was still the main sung service in the morning with a said Holy Communion earlier in the morning. Musically there had been a number of great renderings of the Offices of Morning and Evening Prayer from Byrd and Tomkins, Gibbons and a significant number of others down the ages, including the Gloucester organists whose services are still sung regularly today, Samuel Sebastian Wesley, Sir Herbert Brewer and Herbert Sumsion.

However with an unchanged liturgy organists and composers were largely content to write their music to reflect the type of worship they were familiar with, of which the rather traditional and conservative clergy and congregations would approve. There were exceptions of course, notably C. V. Stanford, whose treatment of the canticles for the Offices was revolutionary in its vigour and excitement. But there was also a great deal of sentimental and trivial music, especially from the nineteenth century, which was sung day in and day out by cathedral choirs who became bored with the routine. As Dr Donald Hunt, a former chorister of Gloucester Cathedral, commented in his book on S. S. Wesley, 'on the whole church music is inclined to be less contemporary than its secular counterparts and quite often, by the time that the new compositional techniques are used, the style has become overworked and outdated'. By the late 1950s, the period during which the lay clerks were becoming elderly and able to cope with only the familiar old music at a reasonably high level, the unique choral heritage of the English Church was a very parochial affair which was having little or no impact. And this was at a time when England had created a new musical culture through the works of Elgar, Vaughan Williams, Walton and Britten. Everyone knew that the Church stood for an old-fashioned cultural ideology.

As we have seen, John was well aware of this as he was of the changes which had become necessary on his appointment as Organist and Choirmaster in 1967. Although, as he once told me, he was traditional in so far as he always composed within the diatonal scale, he made use of modern musical ideas and modulations to express his essential understanding of the words. He was of course in line with a widespread awareness in the Church that change was needed and that worship required a radical revision. The 1960s were a time of social revolution when many customary standards were challenged, not least in music when so many discovered a radical 'pop' music for the first time in which the Beatles became dominant.

Compared with the secular world with its 'flower-power' culture, the new forms of dress, the mini-skirt, a new assessment of moral and social values which heralded the dawn of the 'permissive' society, the Church's first attempt at modernisation was conservative indeed. The Series Two Eucharist was produced in 1965 using the same seventeenth-century language but ordering the service in a more communal way for public worship whereas the old 1662

Anna, John, Janet and Jonathan

service, especially early in the morning, reflected a rather private personal emphasis. While many people received the new service with great relief, an equal number disliked it. However its real importance was that it opened the way for increasingly radical revision during the rest of the century so that church people gradually learned to accept change as an inevitable and necessary way to express their faith in an ever-changing world. For the musicians it offered them a new challenge and opportunity to enrich worship with new settings to the new words.

John's particular gift was that his music was written for the most part with the needs of others in mind. There is a constant, gentle humility which nevertheless penetrates the mind through his music. His liturgical music tends to push the boundaries of consciousness and emotion and to take you into another world, a world he himself was seeking. Rather than disturb you, his music makes you wonder. This was part of John's faith. His Christian belief was not aggressive or assertive, but a thoughtful reflective faith which gave him the freedom to test the boundaries of what is admissible. Nowhere is this more visible than in what has come to be considered as his greatest work, *The Reproaches*.

The Reproaches, compiled by Canon Alan Dunstan, Precentor of Gloucester, were written in 1984 when the revised liturgy for Lent, Holy Week and Easter was introduced into the cathedral. This proved to be an immediate success because it gave a poignancy to and illustrated the pain of the words

> *O my people what wrong have I done to you?*
> *How have I offended you?*
> *Answer me.*

The plainsong and the full choral response is reminiscent of that wonderful *Allegri Miserere, Psalm 51* sung on Ash Wednesday, the first day of Lent and the same atmosphere is caught in *The Reproaches* performed on Good Friday at the end of the penitential season. The work became an instant success, being broadcast on BBC Radio Four on Good Friday 1987, and soon became an established part of the repertoire of many cathedrals in England and overseas.

Specialist musicians will be interested in Anna Turmeau's description of how the 'prayerful word painting' is achieved by use of one of the composer's characteristic 'fingerprints' with a 'falling melodic second interval … as a prime harmonic resource to create rich and magical suspensions and constant points of tension requiring resolution'. She identifies the same use of the falling melodic second interval in his *Requiem* a decade later. She also refers to the 'effective use of suspensions' along with the 'falling melodic second interval' which echoes the technique of Carlo Gesualdo in the closing bars of *O Vos Omnes,* which John himself said inspired him.

The overall effect of *The Reproaches* is quite remarkable, inducing a feeling that one is transported into a medieval world of faith at one moment and then brought back abruptly into the contemporary world of questioning what lies behind the suffering of Christ and of so many others. It seems to sum up the whole meaning of Good Friday for the Christian worshipper.

Another work which has been regularly performed and well loved is the *Requiem*.[4] In view of several well-known and very popular works from Mozart onwards this was perhaps a brave undertaking as it was bound to encourage comparison with the other great and popular twentieth-century compositions such as those by Fauré, Duruflé and

Britten. However the intensity of the emotion along with the great beauty of its cadences make it a memorable experience for anyone who sings or listens to it. The original idea for a *Requiem* grew from a motet which John wrote for the Thanksgiving Service in St Paul's Cathedral in 1996 for Eric Evans who was for many years a canon of the cathedral and Archdeacon of Gloucester before becoming Dean of St Paul's. The following year he was commissioned by Innis Williams to write something as a thanksgiving for the life of her husband, Kenneth and for all the members of the Choral Foundation of Gloucester Cathedral. Canon Neil Heavisides arranged the text, using most of the customary Latin movements but omitting, like Fauré and Duruflé, the *Dies Irae* and *Lacrymosa* and adding as an Offertory a translation of the Russian Cantakion of the Departed and, for the Communion, a poem by John Donne.

John's music has a habit of drawing the participant into a spiritual activity beyond the senses. In her analysis of John's use of harmony and tonality, Anna Turmeau illustrates John's awareness of the quality of individual keys: 'The first 32 bars of the moving *Requiem* remain in the tonic key of C sharp major establishing a powerful aura of prayerfulness' while 'in the final bars of the *Pie Jesu* the tonality rises from D to E major, finally resolving on another of his favourite bright keys, F sharp major, clearly representing the reach for heaven.' The Offertory setting of John Donne's poem moves from a sombre F sharp minor to an exultant A major to bring light to the 'everlasting life'. 'The final Alleluias explode into the suddenly bright tonic major key of B anticipating the key of the following uplifting *Sanctus* movement culminating in *Hosanna in Excelsis* fanfares passing from G major to E major to C major, finally resolving in A major.' Altogether his tonal variations and intricate harmonies suggest that he is writing about relationships, not only of the human relationships which were much on his mind when producing this work but of the relationship between our faltering hopes and the eternal life beyond our understanding.

In John's own words, 'much of the music is based on the original motet; the chord sequences used in this tend to recur throughout the work'. As recorded in the notes provided by Jonathan Sanders for the CD of John's music performed by the choir of Gonville and Caius College, Cambridge under the direction of Geoffrey Webber, John went on to say,

> Overall I have tried to create an atmosphere of light and peace. The only quick movement is the *Sanctus* which was inspired by ringing of bells. The *Pie Jesu* is essentially in the style of a Berceuse and is dedicated to the memory of my first granddaughter Celia, who was born severely disabled in January 1998 and who died aged six months in the following August. In the Offertory, basically a funeral march, I have tried to capture some of the mystery and intensity so typical of Russian Orthodox music. After the *con brio* feeling of the *Sanctus*, the atmosphere of calm and comfort is restored in the *Agnus Dei* and *in Paradisum*.

In view of what we have already heard about John's love of the ancient liturgical words and prayers, it comes as something of a surprise that just after *The Reproaches* were written he admitted that his favourite composition was his song cycle for soprano, clarinet and piano called *In Praise of Gloucestershire*. He considered this his best work and it was obviously close to his heart as he dedicated it to Janet, his wife, and Jonathan and Anna, his son and daughter. It had originally been commissioned by the Stroud Festival.

Much of his secular music was inspired by the county he had come to love, such as his *Gloucestershire Visions*

Dido's first piano lesson

comprising a soprano and tenor solo with full choir and orchestra, commissioned by the Gloucester Choral Society. A smaller work for the Painswick Festival commissioned by Dr James Hoyland, who had played such an important role in the management of the Three Choirs Festival, was *The Beacon* for baritone and piano, based on the ancient history of Painswick with its Stone Age settlement and real beacon which was used to warn the neighbourhood of impending peril.

Other Gloucestershire works provided encouragement for parish church choirs and organists such as Cecil Adams at Dursley. The later anthem *When in our Music God is Glorified* was also written for Dursley amid a number of pieces commissioned by local choral societies and individual friends. Although by the 1990s the Essex boy had become a staunch Gloucestershire lad he did not forget his origins and wrote for the Southend and District Organists' Association as well as the Chester Summer Music Festival, which he had been instrumental in founding.

Like Edward Elgar, John found solace and inspiration when he was able to walk the hills and pastures of the Gloucestershire countryside with his dogs, Dido and Tosca, during his semi-retirement.

His music reflects an important side of his nature. He never forgot his friends or those dear to him. Once John had made a friend, it became a lifelong and loyal friendship. All his family had their special mention in his musical dedications, among them Jonathan and Caroline with their little daughter Celia (*Via Lucis*), Talia, a granddaughter (*Sing we merrily*), Silas, a grandson (*Insight – For Unaccompanied Double Choir*) and possibly most poignantly of all, a memorial to his mother, who had been the only remaining family relation with whom he was in contact. Many of his friends felt that they could contact him to commission special music and some pieces came out of the pure friendship.

Reflecting on his life and work John constantly admitted that he didn't like the modern language services very much, in spite of composing a very lively and much-loved congregational accompaniment to the revised Eucharist. He thought they did not fit the atmosphere and architectural symbolism of the great cathedrals although he allowed that they might have some worth in a more intimate setting:

> In a cathedral you have got to have a spacious liturgy and spacious language. Everything goes a bit slower because of the space. I find using the modern words does provide fresh inspiration, and I'm not against using them, but I don't like them as much as the old words! In a way the older words are easier to set to music; some of the rhythms in the modern settings of the liturgy don't honestly lend

themselves to music. Sometimes they are, well, too 'chat-
tery' and colloquial.

As far as his own rules of composition were concerned, John
was always intensely keen to consider those for whom he
was writing, and was never content to do it for his own pleas-
ure and interest. He once told me that some modern
composers have no concern for the limitations of the human
voice and expect singers to pick out notes from out of the
ether as if they were instrumentalists. He was insistent that
you must offer the singer a way in to the note and that cathedral choirs in particular carry a very heavy daily load of
music which has to be learned and sung. 'If you want to
write things for the Church, you've got to write things which
are, hopefully, fresh, but at the same time, not too demanding technically.' He also said that he found his inspiration
mostly with sacred words and 'in general I'm not much good
at writing music without words'. Roy Massey summed up
John's approach to composition: 'His music reflects the
instinctive knowledge of what the voice and choir can do
and is superbly crafted to this end. When writing for instruments his orchestration is colourful and carefully balanced.'

That said, worthy of special mention is a popular album of
piano and organ music which John edited, *The Gloucester
Organ Album*. It consists of works for organ written by six
Gloucester organists: S. S. Wesley, C. H. Lloyd, C. L. Williams,
Herbert Brewer, Herbert Sumsion and John Sanders. Not
only is the editing of the music done with the meticulous
accuracy and detail we came to expect of him, but his own
contribution, a *Toccata in C*, is an early masterly work,
written in his relatively young days of composing in 1978. It
is a robust and startling work with a stream of sometimes
dissonant arpeggios which end in a tumultuously resound-

ing climax. Of it he wrote, 'It has a key – albeit a modal version of D minor – and a tune! When writing a Toccata one is uncontrollably afflicted by French influences for which I make no apology.' It suggests that he was over-modest about his ability as a writer of instrumental music although the output was small by comparison with his choral works.

John was at his happiest when composing for well-known and familiar prayerful words and it is fitting to complete this chapter with two prayers in which his music takes the traditional words to the brink of mystery. The first is Cardinal Newman's prayer which has been widely used in churches, colleges, schools and wherever prayers are said, for more than a century:

> *O Lord, support us all the day long of this troublous life,*
> *until the shades lengthen and the evening comes,*
> *the busy world is hushed, and the fever of life is over,*
> *and our work done.*
> *Then, Lord, in thy mercy grant us safe lodging,*
> *an holy rest and peace at the last,*
> *through Jesus Christ our Lord.*
> *Amen.*

John's setting was commissioned by the churchwardens of St Margaret's Church, Westminster Abbey to recognise the work of Simon Over who was Director of Music from 1992–2002. Again we hear those delicious dissonances in the chords expressing this *troublous* life and the *fever* of life and overall it becomes a prayer of great hope rather than a regretful time of old age.

Our final work is also the last piece of music John wrote before he went into hospital for the last time. It is appropriately composed for a prayer written by F. W. Harvey, who was a Gloucester chorister and companion of Ivor Gurney in the time of Sir Herbert Brewer. Both served in the First World War, Harvey being decorated with the Distinguished Conduct Medal before being taken prisoner. It was in the Prisoner of War camp that Harvey wrote his best known poem, *Ducks*. This not only became a favourite poem in the English-speaking world but was also a set poem for German boys and girls studying for their Abitur examinations before and after the Second World War. Harvey and Gurney both became known as war poets. After his release from POW camp, Harvey returned to Gloucester, working as a solicitor by the front entrance of King's School House and became immersed in the beauty and life of his beloved county. The River Severn had a particular appeal to him with 'its sweet shape and winding river'. As Jonathan Sanders wrote, 'there is a real sense of calm and peace in the setting of this beautiful valedictory text'.

> *O Lord, within my heart for ever*
> *Set this sweet shape and winding river,*
> *That I may taste their comfort till I die,*
> *And feed upon them in eternity.*

Epilogue

John Sanders retired as Organist and Master of the Choristers at Gloucester rather earlier than might have been expected, at the age of sixty. His main reason for doing so was that he wanted to spend time composing in order to leave something permanent for his legacy as a church musician. He was also suffering from a lifetime's conducting with

John on receiving his Lambeth Doctorate, with the Most Reverend Robert Runcie, Archbishop of Canterbury, 1990

a very painful right shoulder and arm, probably originating from a previous illness, and he felt increasingly that he could not do justice to the demanding work. Nevertheless he continued as Director of Music at the Ladies' College for some years.

Adopting a lifestyle reminiscent of Elgar, John was then able to enjoy, with Janet and the dogs Dido and Tosca, the exploration of his beloved Gloucestershire and Herefordshire countryside where he found such inspiration for his compositions. Unlike Messien he did not particularly respond to the natural sounds of the woods and fields but caught the mood of the implacable, gentle and unthreatening atmosphere in which he found himself. There is an essential serenity in his music which relates to the pastoral surroundings. But he was always quick to say that the inspiration derived from the countryside and from his friends and admirers who commissioned his works amounted to only five per cent of the working of the composition. The other ninety-five per cent involved perspiration and hard thinking.

The notion that his composing years in retirement marked a gentle retreat is far from the truth. Melodies were running around his brain, ideas had to be analysed and resolved, deadlines were to be met. Also for John it was always important to put himself into the minds of those who commissioned and were to perform his works. He was careful to match the sophistication of his pieces to the nature and ability of the performers.

Before his retirement John once told me that he was not looking forward to retirement outside the Cathedral Close because it might mean having to put up with indifferent music in a struggling parish church. The very thought of it was off-putting. Perhaps inevitably he became organist at Upton Bishop, at least on a part-time basis, and the parishioners could scarcely believe their luck. However he did not take over entirely and ensured that the established organist continued to have a part to play. Less inevitable was his becoming treasurer of the parochial church council, an unenviable job at the best of times and one which is not particularly sought after. However his experience of keeping meticulous records of his own accounts and the speed with which he reminded his publishers about the royalties owing to him indicate that he was well qualified to supervise the parish finances.

For a well-loved, practical and popular musician there is little opportunity for real retirement and, at times, it must have seemed to John that he had begun a new full-time career. Not only was he constantly at work on new commissions, but he remained much in demand in the diocese and beyond for his advice and practical assistance. During the crisis when his successor in Gloucester, David Briggs, suffered a heart attack, John was called in to help out. Right up to the end he was in the habit of working a fifty- or sixty-hour week.

John loved a party and rejoiced in meeting old and new friends in convivial surroundings. It was thus appropriate that Janet should celebrate his 70th birthday by organising three parties, on the 23rd, 29th and 30th November 2003, involving so many friends from school days to his retirement at Upton Bishop. With hindsight it was a remarkably fortuitous event enabling John to celebrate his life's work in his favourite company.

Some three weeks later, he went into hospital in Hereford for what is now regarded as a routine operation for a hip replacement. It still involves major surgery which requires a robust constitution. As it happened there was a serious complication and John was rushed to the intensive care unit at Nevill Hall, Abergavenny, there being no vacant bed in the County Hospital in Hereford. He was returned to Hereford a day or two later, but alas the body could not cope with the travel or the surgery and he died shortly before Christmas, on 23rd December.

After a simple family funeral at Upton Bishop his shocked friends were invited to a memorial service in Gloucester Cathedral on 28th February 2004. The cathedral was absolutely full half an hour before the service began and many had to stand at the back and in the aisles. One estimate given to me was that some 1400 people attended. The service was Evensong from the 1662 Prayer Book which John so loved. Andrew Nethsingha, Organist and Director of Music at the cathedral, conducted the choir and, fittingly, two former assistant organists, Mark Blatchly and Mark Lee, played before the service began, along with the current assistant, Robert Houssart. At the end of the service the voluntary for which the whole congregation remained was played by Dr Roy Massey. Perhaps one of the most numinous parts of the service came after the opening voluntaries when there was a shared, deep silence. We were able to recall John's words, 'Music begins with silence ... You can only fully appreciate the beauty and effect of music when it grows out of silence.' The silence was broken by the music to the words of F. W. Harvey's poem, quoted in the last chapter. The now well-known Sanders *Responses* conveyed the liturgy, which also included Psalms 122 and 150 sung to John's chants and ended with John's *Dresden Amen*. The *Magnificat* and *Nunc Dimittis* were sung to Howell's *Gloucester Service* so loved by John while the congregation were able to celebrate his whole-hearted and generous life when the choir sang one of his earliest and most triumphant works, the *Festival Te Deum*.

During his lifetime John was awarded the greatest honours a musician can receive. With characteristic modesty and humility he was heard to say after receiving a Lambeth Doctor of Music in 1990, 'Well, at least I haven't let the side down', and his contribution to the music of the Church was further acknowledged by the award of an OBE in 1994. Following a letter of congratulation from Peter Hillier, chairman of the Choral Society throughout John's time, he wrote:

> Janet and I are delighted as the citation reads, 'For service to music'. I am therefore assuming that it does not relate to any particular facet of my work and am therefore regarding it not merely as recognition for me but for all the organisations with which I have been associated during my thirty-three years in Gloucestershire: The Cathedral, The Ladies' College, the King's School, the Three Choirs Festival, the Choral Society and the Symphony Orchestra, the Music Society, the Royal School of Church Music, the Organists' Association, the Saint Cecilia Singers and perhaps for my work as composer. All much enjoyed.

Further honours came from his old music college when he was created a Fellow of the Royal College of Music and an honorary Fellow of the Royal School of Church Music.

Beyond his outstanding musical ability, those who worked with John and knew him as a colleague and friend were constantly aware of his unfailing courtesy and his absolute personal and professional integrity. The fourteen hundred or so people who attended his memorial service were there to join in a general thanksgiving for the life and work of a profoundly unobtrusive Christian gentleman who lived and gave his all for his family, his music, and his duty to God in the *Opus Dei* which he took so naturally yet so seriously. As one obituarist put it, 'John was a thoughtful, highly intelligent, kindly and humorous person with a great gift for friendship. He was a loving husband and father and in Janet he had a wife in a million. He loved his fellow men and they loved him in return.' From those early years when the thirteen-year-old Rod Hunter recognised John Sanders as a person he wanted to know as a friend, so many people who came into contact with him came to look upon him as their friend for life.

Appendix One

The Organ of Gloucester Cathedral[1]

Dr Arthur Hill, a Victorian expert on organ cases, dated the case of the Chaire organ facing on to the Choir at 1579. Although there must have been an organ installed at this time any records of a medieval organ or indeed a Tudor one have been lost. However many of the pipes in the present instrument date from 1663 and were incorporated into the organ completed in 1666 by Thomas Harris who also built the main case.

The painting on the display pipes was done by a local artist, John Campion. On the west side the crowned initials of Charles II appear and on the east side are the arms of the Duke of York and the Earl of Clarendon. The arms of Dean Brough and the six prebendaries of the day are on the Chaire case. The organ was placed in a loft above the Choir Stalls in the South Transept and was not moved to its position on the Screen until 1718.

During the next centuries several modifications were made, the main one being by 'Father Willis', who in 1888 and 1898 added extra stops and enlarged the cases. In 1920, following a scheme of Sir Herbert Brewer, Cathedral Organist, Harrison and Harrison modernised the organ in the popular 'orchestral' fashion of the time.

John Sanders realised in 1968 that the time had come for a major overhaul and directed the work done by William Hill and Son and Norman and Beard with Ralph Downes as designer and consultant. The case was returned to a free-standing position away from the parapet and renovated by the expert picture restorer Anne Plowden. Tonally there was a return to the purer and more traditional sound in preference to the 'orchestral' and 'romantic' nineteenth-century sound with the façade pipes being made to speak again. The whole instrument was contained within the case but is able to speak with equal effect into Nave and Choir.

The Organ in 1670

Great		**Choir**	
Open Diapason (East)	8	Stopped Diapason	8
Open Diapason (West)	8	Principal	4
Stopped Diapason	8	Flute	4
Principal	4	Fifteenth	2
Twelfth	2 2/3	Vox Humana	8
Fifteenth	2		
Sexquialtera	IV		
Cornet (from c)	V		
Trumpet	8		

Swell			
Open Diapason	8	Cornet	III
Stopped Diapason	8	Trumpet	8
Principal	4	Hautboy	8

(Wooden pedal pipes were added by Bishop in 1831)

The Organ in 1971

Four Manuals C to a, 58 notes

Pedals, C to g, 32 notes

H = stops incorporating Harris pipes, 1670

Great

Gedecktpommer	16
Open Diapason (East) H	8
Open Diapason (West) H	8
Spitzflute (West)	8
Bourdon(H)	8
Octave(East)H	4
Prestant (West)H	4
Stopped Flute	4
Flageolet	2
Quartane (West) H	2 2/3
Mixture IV–VI H	4
Cornet IV (from c)	4
Posaune	8
Trumpet	4
Clarion	4

Pedal

Principal H ext.	16
Flute (wood)	16
Sub Bass	16
Octave H	8
Stopped Flute	8
Choral Bass	4
Open Flute	2
Mixture IV	2 2/3
Bombarde	16
Trumpet	8
Shawm	4

Choir

Stopped Diapason	8
Principal H	4
Chimney Flute	4
Fifteenth	2
Nazard	1 2/3
Sesquialtera II	1 1/3-2 1/3
Mixture III	1/2
Cremona	8
Tremulant	

Swell

Chimney Flute	8
Salicional	8
Celeste	8
Principal	4
Open Flute	4
Nazard	2 2/3
Gemshorn	2
Tierce	1 3/5
Mixture IV	1
Cimbel III	1/5
Fagotto	16
Trumpet	8
Hautboy	8
Vox Humana	8
Tremulant	

West Positive

Gedecktpommer	8	Tierce	1 3/4
Spitzflute	4	Larigot	1 1/3
Nazard	2 2/3	Cimbel III	1/2
Doublette	2	Tremulant	

Unison couplers, and Sub-Octave to Great West flues.
Transfers of Great reeds and West Great flues to Manual IV.
Electro-pneumatic and electro-magnetic actions.

Appendix Two

List of Works
by John Sanders

Number	Date	Title	Forces	Commission/Dedication	Publisher
1	1958	*My Beloved Spake*	SATB	For the wedding of Andrew and Pauline Taylor	Unpublished
2	1960	*Festival Te Deum*	SATB + Organ/Full orchestra	For the Cheltenham Bach Choir	OUP – reverted to JDS
3	1965	*Welcome Yule*	Baritone solo, SATB Choir + Organ	–	Unpublished
4	1971	*Soliloquy*	Organ	For Cecil Adams, Dursley Parish Church	Cramer
5	1978	*A Carol for Today*	SATB + Organ (SAB version also available)	–	Ramsey / Banks
6	1978	*Responses*	SATB unaccomp	–	Oecumuse – reverted to JDS?
7	1979	*Toccata*	Organ	–	Novello
8	1982	*Te Deum*	SSA + Organ (+ optional trpt and percussion)	Commissioned by Cheltenham Ladies' College	Novello
9	1986	*Jubilate Deo*	SATB + Organ/Full orchestra	–	Roger Dean (Elkin)
10	1988	*In Praise of Gloucestershire*	Soprano, Clarinet and Piano (arranged for Soprano, Clarinet, Harp and Strings in 2003) [Song cycle]	Commissioned by the Stroud Festival, dedicated to Janet, Anna and Jonathan	Unpublished
11	1989	*What Child is This?*	SATB unaccomp	–	Unpublished

Number	Date	Title	Forces	Commission/Dedication	Publisher
12	1989	*Day by Day*	SATB + Organ	–	Roger Dean (Elkin)
13	1989	*Responses*	SATB/RSCM		
14	1989	*Prayer of St Francis*	SATB + Organ	For the choir of the Gloucester Royal Hospital	Roger Dean (Elkin)
15	1990	*St Mark Passion*	SATB unaccomp	Dedicated to Gloucester Cathedral Choir	RSCM
16	1990	*Tomorrow Shall Be My Dancing Day*	SATB unaccomp	–	Roger Dean (Elkin)
17	1991	*Teach us, Good Lord, to Serve Thee*	SATB + Organ	For the choirs of the Gloucester Royal Hospital and Nairobi Cathedral	RSCM
18	1991	*An Easter Carol*	SATB unaccomp	For Arnold Pugh and the Choir of Rugby Parish Church	Roger Dean (Elkin)
19	1991	*A Canticle of Joy*	SS + Organ	For Neil Shroff and the Auckland Boys' Choir	Roger Dean (Elkin)
20	1992	*O Praise God*	SAB Choir + Organ	–	Kevin Mayhew
21	1992	*Hymns for RSCM*	SATB	–	RSCM
22	1992	*Fierce Raged the Tempest*	SATB + Organ	Commissioned by the Southend and District Organists' Association, dedicated to the musicians of the Borough	McCrimmon
23	1993	*Reproaches*	SATB unaccomp	For Alan Dunstan	RSCM
24	1993	*A Star Shining in the East*	SATB Choir and Organ	Commissioned by the Salisbury Dicesan Church Music Committee	Unpublished

Number	Date	Title	Forces	Commission/Dedication	Publisher
25	1993	*The Beacon*	Baritone solo and Piano [Song Cycle]	Commissioned by James Hoyland for the Painswick Festival	Unpublished
26	1993	*Whence is That Goodly Fragrance?*	SATB + Organ (SAB, SSA versions also available)	–	Kevin Mayhew
27	1993	*The Creator*	SATB + Organ	For the wedding of Jonathan and Caroline	Presser (Kalmus) – reverted back to JAS
28	1994	*Blessed be That Maid Mary*	SATB unaccomp	–	Roger Dean (Elkin)
29	1995	*Oculi Omnium* (revised)	SATB unaccomp	For the Choir of Fitzwilliam College, Cambridge	Unpublished
30	1995	*Anthem of the Incarnation*	SSA Semi-chorus, SATB Choir + Organ	Commissioned by Peter Lacey for Ian Fox and the King's School Choir, Gloucester	Unpublished
31	1995	*Gloucestershire Visions*	Soprano and Tenor solo, SATB, Full orchestra [Cantata]	Commissioned by Gloucester Choral Society in memoriam Ursula Alcock	Unpublished
32	1995	*The Cotswolds*	Mezzo soprano and Baritone solos, Childrens' semi-chorus, SATB Choir + Full orchestra [Cantata]	Commissioned by Stroud Choral Society	Unpublished
33	1996	*Psalm 150 of Four Festal Psalms*	SATB + Organ	–	OUP

Number	Date	Title	Forces	Commission/Dedication	Publisher
34	1996	*Magnificat and Nunc Dimittis* (Hereford)	SATB + Organ	Dedicated to Roy Massey and the Choir of Hereford Cathedral	Encore
35	1996	*The Brisk Young Widow*	Soprano and Tenor or solo, SATB Choir unaccomp	For Mark Lee and the St Cecilia Singers	Unpublished
36	1996	*Requiem* (single movement)	SATB unaccomp	In memory of Eric Evans, and dedicated to Linda, Alex and Georgie	Unpublished
37	1996	*Here We Come A-Wassailing*	Unpublished	–	Unpublished
38	1996	*Magnificat & Nunc Dimittis* (Gloucester)	Treble and Bass solos, SATB Choir + Organ	Commissioned by the Chapter and Old Choristers' Association of Gloucester Cathedral, dedicated to the memory of the composer's mother	Encore
39	1997	*Coelos Ascendit Hodie*	SATB unaccomp	Dedicated to Brian and Hilary Cookson	Kirklees Music
40	1997	*Welcome Yule*	SATB unaccomp	For Rebecca	Unpublished
41	1997	*King of Glory*	SA + Organ	Commissioned by Ian Hiller, St George's School, Ascot, dedicated to Janet	Encore
42	1997	*The Call*	SAB + Organ	–	Kevin Mayhew
43	1997	*Canticum Dei*	SATB + organ	For Jonathan Hadfield	Unpublished

Number	Date	Title	Forces	Commission/Dedication	Publisher
44	1997	*Deus Misereatur*	SATB + Organ	Commissioned by John Brooks to mark the retirement of Dr Anthony Crossland	Sacred Music Press (Roger Dean?)
45	1998	*Mass of the Creator*	SATB + Organ	Dedicated to Joan Wake Cleveland	Unpublished
46	1998	*Via Lucis*	Tenor and Baritone solos, SATB Choir + Full orchestra [Cantata]	Commissioned by Monmouth Choral Society, dedicated to Jonathan, Caroline and their daughter	Unpublished
47	1998	*Requiem*	SATB, unaccomp	Commissioned in thanksgiving for the life of Kenneth Williams and all former members of the Choral Foundation at Gloucester Cathedral	Encore
48	1998	*Celebremus*	SATB Choir + Full orchestra	Commissioned by Jersey Instrumental Music Service, dedicated to Brian Grady	Unpublished
49	1999	*The Firmament*	Treble solo, SATB Choir, Organ	Commissioned by Coutts Bank for Marcus Huxley and the Choir of Birmingham Cathedral	Unpublished
50	1999	*Jubilate*	SSAA + Organ/Piano	Commissioned by Cheltenham Ladies' College, dedicated to memory of Sheila Cranshaw	Unpublished
51	1999	*Psalm 121*	SATB + Organ	Written for wedding of Anna and Jon	Encore

Number	Date	Title	Forces	Commission/Dedication	Publisher
52	2000	*Oculi Omnium*	Soprano and Contralto solos, SATB, unaccomp	Commissioned by Ruth and Jean Hooper	Encore
53	2000	*Millenium Suite*	Full orchestra	Commissioned by the Hereford Youth Orchestra	Unpublished
54	2000	*The Roads* (and others?)	Baritone solo and Piano	Dedicated to Mark Wildman	Unpublished
55	2000	*Come My Way*	SATB + Organ	For Christopher Barton and the Choir of St Woolos Cathedral	Encore
56	2000	*Sing We Merrily*	Treble solo, SATB Choir 1, SSA Choir 2, Organ	Commissioned jointly by the Chester Summer Music Festival and Chester Cathedral, Dedicated to Talia (grand-daughter)	Unpublished
57	2000	*Insight*	SSAATTBB unaccomp	Dedicated to Silas (grandson)	Unpublished
58	2000	*Songs of the Hills*	Soprano and Baritone + Full orchestra [Song cycle]	Dedicated to the Gloucestershire Symphony Orchestra past & present, remembering especially Michael Gryspeerdt	Unpublished
59	2001	*My Beloved Spake* (revised)	SSAATTBB		Banks
60	2001	*O Sing Joyfully*	SATB + Organ	Dedicated to David on his 40th Birthday	Unpublished
61	2001	*Petite Suite Anglaise*	Solo violin	Commissioned by and written for Jim Coles	Unpublished

Number	Date	Title	Forces	Commission/Dedication	Publisher
62	2001	*When in our Music God is Glorified*	SATB + Organ	To Nigel Davies and the Choir of Dursley Parish Church	Unpublished
63	2001	*Urbs Beata*	Alto solo, SATB Choir, Solo Cello, Brass ensemble, Percussion and Organ [Cantata]	Commissioned by Gloucester Three Choirs Festival	Unpublished
64	2002	*Everyone Sang*	Soprano solo, SATB unaccomp	Commissioned by Pamela White to celebrate the 25th Anniversary of the Britten Singers, dedicated to the musicians of Herefordshire, past and present	Banks
65	2002	*Cradle Song*	Cello + Piano	Dedicated to Jamie (grandson)	Unpublished
66	2002	*When Heart Meets Heart*	Soprano + Piano [Song cycle]	Commissioned in memory of Roland Pepper, dedicated to Anna and Jon	Unpublished
67	2002	*Thou Art the Way*	SATB + Organ	For Glyn Martin, Paul Babbedge and the Choir of Holy Trinity Church, Northwood	Unpublished
68	2002	*The Age of Herbert and Vaughan*	Soprano solo, Treble Recorder, Cello and Harpsichord	Dedicated to Percy Young on his 90th Birthday	Unpublished
69	2002	*Quam Dilecta*	SSAATTBB unaccomp	For Michael Guest, Lichfield Cathedral	Unpublished
70	2002	*Carol of the Advent*	SSA unaccomp	Commissioned by St George's School, Ascot	RSCM

Number	Date	Title	Forces	Commission/Dedication	Publisher
71	2002	*Magnificat and Nunc Dimittis* (Lichfield)	SSAATTBB unaccomp	For the Choir of Lichfield Cathedral, to celebrate Percy Young's 90th birthday	Encore
72	2002	*Lament*	Cello + Piano	For Juliet Tomlinson	Encore
73	2003	*Dedication*	SATB + Piano/Organ	For Simon and Ruth on their wedding day	Unpublished
74	2003	*O Lord, Support us All the Day Long*	SATB, unaccomp	Commissioned by the wardens of St Margaret's Church, Westminster Abbey for Simon Over	Encore
75	2003	*Mandatum Novum*	SATB + Organ	Commissioned by Neil Heavisides for the Royal Maundy Service, Gloucester Cathedral	Unpublished
76	2003	*Missa Beata Maria Virgine*	Alternatim Mass for SATB Choir and People + Organ (Douai Abbey)	Commissioned by her family to commemorate the life of work of Judy Bullock, dedicated to Jude (grandson)	Unpublished
77	2003	*Et Incarnatus Est*	SATB unaccomp	Dedicated to John Rowntree and the Choir of Douai Abbey	Unpublished
78	2003	*A Prayer*	SATB + Organ	For John Mitchell, Dedicated to Kiera (Granddaughter)	Encore

Appendix Three

The Sanders Society

'As Organist and Master of the Choristers of Gloucester
Cathedral and Conductor of the Three Choirs Festival
for over a quarter of a century, John Sanders
enriched the world of music far beyond the normal
confines of the provincial organ loft. Organist,
conductor, composer, teacher, adjudicator and not
least an assiduous administrator, this multi-faceted
musician influenced and nurtured the lives of many
generations of aspiring musicians.'

Kenneth Shenton, *The Independent*,
31st December 2003

In recognition of John's achievements in pursuing his lifelong career in the service of music and especially that of the
cathedral, the Sanders Society has been founded with the
following aims:

a) To promote the music of John Sanders.
b) To support choral music for the liturgy.
c) To encourage young composers to maintain the cathedral
   choral tradition.

To achieve the third aim The John Sanders Memorial

Competition for Young Composers has been established as a triennial competition for composers under the age of 28. Works of about eight minutes' length for SATB choirs, suitable for performance at Evensong are invited. The winning composition will be sung by Gloucester Cathedral Choir and other performances will be arranged with twelve choirs of other eminent cathedrals who have agreed to participate.

Further details of the Society's membership and activities may be obtained from

The Sanders Society,
144 Tuffley Avenue,
Gloucester GL1 5NS.

Notes

Chapter One

1. I am very grateful to Mr Rod Hunter who gave me a great deal of information about Felsted School and John Sanders' time there.
2. From the archives of Felsted School, including a brief history of the evacuation to Herefordshire.
3. From an interview recorded by John Brooks. This invaluable source recorded John's own thoughts about the development of his life.
4. Interview with John Brooks.
5. Felsted archives.
6. Felsted in Herefordshire.
7. Recollections of Rod Hunter.
8. Obituary of George Thorne – Felsted Archives.
9. Reminiscences of Lt. Gen. Sir Peter Beale and from his memorial service address.
10. Felsted school magazine.

Chapter Two

1. I owe this outline of Sir John Dykes Bower's biography to Terence Gilmore-James, a pupil of his.
2. Interview by John Brooks.
3. From Lt. Gen. Sir Peter Beale.
4. From the records of Gonville and Caius College, Cambridge.
5. From Sir Peter Beale and the sleeve of Gonville and Caius' recording of excerpts from Gilbert and Sullivan.
6. Interview by John Brooks and Sir Peter Beale's reminiscences.
7. From an article in CAM magazine.
8. Interview with John Brooks.
9. Rod Hunter's recollections.
10. Rod Hunter's recollections.
11. Interview by John Brooks.

Chapter Three
1. The King's School magazine.
2. I am grateful to Mr Emrys Evans who supplied me with many details of John's years as Director of Music of the King's School and assistant organist. Mr Evans was a master at the King's School, contemporary with John.
3. From Suzanne Eward's history of Gloucester Close in Stuart times, *No Fine but a Glass of Wine*, published by Michael Russell, page 97.
4. Ibid., page 17.
5. Ibid., page 18f.
6. Ibid., page 217.
7. From *Three Choirs* by Anthony Boden, published by Alan Sutton.
8. From *Samuel Sebastian Wesley* by Donald Hunt, published by Seren Books, page 51
9. Ibid., page 52.
10. From a conversation with Emrys Evans.

Chapter Four
1. Letter to Dean and Chapter, Chester Cathedral in Chester Record Office.
2. Dean and Chapter records.
3. Dean and Chapter records.
4. Specifications and estimates from Walker and Son and Rushworth and Dreaper. I am grateful to Philip Rushworth who kindly gave me access to the choir records of Chester Cathedral. He did tell me that his predecessor Roger Fisher was glad that John's restoration had not been carried out but a more modest improvement was made to the organ shortly after his departure.
5. Janet Walker and her husband, long-standing members of Chester Choral Society, provided me with this and other details of John's life there.
6. From Martin Cooke, still chairman of the Chester Music Festival.
7. Ian Terrett, organist, provided this information.
8. Much of the history of the Music Festival is drawn from notes by David Laing for the Festival Programme in 1966 when it was restored.

Chapter Five
1. *The King's School, Gloucester* shown on ITV in 1985, produced by Dilys Howell.
2. From *God and Music* by J. Harrington Edwards, published by J. M. Dent, 1904.
3. From the ITV programme.

4. Interview by John Brooks.
5. William (Bill) Armiger has been a constant support in the writing of this book. He is currently chairman and organiser of the Sanders Society.
6. *Friends of Cathedral Music* Magazine.
7. I was on this tour but I am grateful for Mark Blatchly's article in *Choir Schools Today* for several apposite reflections.
8. From a video of the Choral Society dinner, kindly loaned by Peter Hillier, long-serving chairman of the Society.
9. From the ITV programme.

Chapter Six
1. Anthony Boden, *Three Choirs*, page 13
2. Ibid., page 19.
3. From John Sanders' correspondence.
4. Anthony Boden, op.cit.
5. For the story of the *Mass of Christ the King*, I am grateful to Anthony Boden and John's correspondence as well as *Citizen* newspaper reports.
6. Much of the information in this chapter is drawn from the Three Choirs Gloucester programmes as well as personal reminiscences.
7. Barry Still, the *Guardian*, 28th August 1986.

Chapter Seven
1. The source material of John's compositions was found in his voluminous correspondence, kindly loaned by Mrs Janet Sanders.
2. Anna Turmeau produced an exhaustive study of some of John's most significant works as part of a degree dissertation. She is frequently quoted in this chapter and I am sorry I have been unable to track her down.
3. Lorenz publishers have published much of John's work in the USA and sold it through an agent in England.
4. The *Requiem* is included in the CD produced by Priory for the British Composer Series 1. The choir of Gonville and Caius College, Cambridge directed by Geoffrey Webber perform eleven of John Sanders' works. The notes about the pieces are mostly by John himself, compiled by Jonathan Sanders.

Appendix One
1. The details of Gloucester Cathedral Organ are abridged from *The Gloucester Organ Album* edited by John Sanders and published by Novello in 1979. I am grateful for their permission to reproduce the material.

Index of Names

Lightning Source UK Ltd.
Milton Keynes UK
UKOW030921151211

183840UK00001B/28/P